100 THINGS TO DO IN CANADA BEFORE YOU DIE

ROGERS CENTRE

100 THINGS TO DO IN CANADA BEFORE YOU DIE

SHERI McDONALD

Reedy Press
PO Box 5131
St. Louis, MO 63139, USA
www.reedypress.com

Library of Congress Control Number: 2019936720

ISBN: 9781681062303

Design by Jill Halpin

All images courtesy of Sheri McDonald unless otherwise noted.

Printed in the United States of America
19 20 21 22 23   5 4 3 2 1

Please note that websites, phone numbers, addresses, and company names are subject to change or cancellation. We did our best to relay the most accurate information available, but due to circumstances beyond our control, please do not hold us liable for misinformation. When exploring new destinations, please do your homework before you go.

DEDICATION

I dedicate this book to two very special friends who had important roles in my travel writing career.

To Cheryl, who embraced a partnership with me for a print magazine that we ran for several years. Without her, I wouldn't have taken that first flight or learned the intricacies of print publications and advertising that have helped me so much as a travel writer.

Also, to Suzi, my oldest friend (not in age!), who encouraged me to start my own blog and helped me along the way, which eventually brought me to travel writing. We could not have guessed where this would go, but it certainly would not have landed here without her help.

CONTENTS

Food and Drink

Sports and Recreation

History and Culture

PREFACE

In the summer of 2010, I started a parenting blog called Kidsumers, which quickly evolved into a family travel and food blog. A few years later I created a site called Family enRoute that is dedicated to family travel. These blogs opened the door for me to explore North America and the Caribbean with my family, something I never dreamed I would do.

Having boarded my first airplane at the age of thirty-six, the travel bug hit me a little later in life than most. Even if I started a little late, I am so grateful that I realized the value of experiencing other customs and cultures. I believe that travel is the best teacher, and I'm grateful that my children are growing up as explorers. I am especially excited to help them understand their Canadian roots by sharing this great country with them.

Narrowing down my list of *100 Things to Do in Canada Before You Die* was a difficult task. I decided to focus on a list that defines Canadian roots and values across the provinces and territories. The list is for Canadians who are exploring their own backyards as well as international visitors who aren't as familiar with the country. This book is a mixture of well-known attractions and some off-the-beaten-path ideas, and I have tried to ensure there is something for everyone.

I hope that readers will use my book as a starting point for traveling the Great White North. Every city, town, and province has a unique story to tell through the people, the land, and the attractions. Take pause on your travels, meet the locals, and embrace their stories.

ACKNOWLEDGMENTS

I would like to thank Josh Stevens from Reedy Press Inc. for taking a chance on me when I shot him an email out of the blue, suggesting he take his Before You Die series into Canada. The team at Reedy Press Inc. has been supportive, encouraging, and wonderful to work with.

Thank you to my husband, Michael, and children, Eric, Kellen, Avery, and Griffin, who share my love of travel and tolerated my need for quiet to write. A very special thank-you to my mother, Ruth, who has made some of my travel possible and always supported my endeavours. I was proud to have her at my side for that first flight (for her as well) and for other trips throughout the years.

Destinations, hotels, attractions, and fellow travelers have helped me discover so many amazing parts of Canada. Various travel writers have offered their assistance and shared their experiences through emails, blog posts, and videos. Without them, we would have a very different list, so I am grateful for their input.

Lastly, I would like to thank everyone who has read my stories and interacted with me through social media. Your continued support is what keeps me writing.

EXPERIENCES AND EVENTS

OBSERVE
NATURE'S LIGHT SHOW

Crisp fresh air, northern hospitality, and a light show like no other is what you will find in Aurora Village. A circle of teepees offer respite from the cold in this remote village in the Northwest Territories. Sleigh-like seats are heated for comfort and provide a 360-degree viewing experience. Located under the aurora oval, a halo-like ring around the North Pole, Aurora Village is one of the best viewing areas in the world. The dark winter days and absence of artificial light create the perfect environment to see the aurora borealis up to 240 nights a year.

The aurora borealis, also known as the northern lights, is a natural light show of epic proportions that takes place when gaseous particles from the earth and sun collide. When this phenomenon occurs, curtains of colourful lights dance through the northern sky. They can appear as yellow, green, purple, and even pink ribbons of light.

Yellowknife, NT X1A 2P4
1-867-669-0006
auroravillage.com

FUN FACT

Vehicle license plates in the Northwest Territories are shaped like polar bears.

2

FLY
TO THE YUKON ICEFIELDS

Few people have the privilege of taking in the vast beauty of the Yukon icefields from above, but it is a unique experience that has been dubbed "flightseeing." A ski plane takes you over acres of forests and above turquoise lakes that reflect the clouds. The towering snow-capped mountains surround flat white fields of ice and snow. Your tour will take you near and around remarkable mountains, such as Mount Logan and Mount St. Elias, as well as many others, before landing at Kluane National Park to explore the largest non-polar icefield in the world. Walking in such a remote part of the world near mystical blue glaciers and over fields of ice is a surreal experience that you won't soon forget. For an even more advanced experience, spend a few nights at Icefield Discovery Camp.

1-867-841-4204
icefielddiscovery.com

FUN FACT
Carcross Desert in the Yukon is the smallest desert in the world at only one square mile.

3

WATCH STORMS
IN UCLUELET

If you are drawn to the vigor of a storm and your soul is soothed by the sound of waves crashing onto the shore, Ucluelet, British Columbia, is the place to visit. Ucluelet (pronounced yew-*kloo*-let) sits off the west coast of Vancouver Island and is surrounded by the Pacific Rim National Park Reserve. Nature's fury shows up in Ucluelet in the form of ten to fifteen mega-storms each season. From November to March, the area withstands brute force winds that can move at more than seventy kilometres an hour. The fifteen- to twenty-five-foot-high waves batter the coast, leaving treasures of the sea behind for zealous beachcombers.

Storm watchers can take in the show from the safety of the indoors or strap on some rubber boots and rain gear to feel the true power of Mother Nature. Consult the locals for safety tips before going near the rocks or on the beach and avoid a Mary Poppins situation by leaving the umbrella behind.

discoverucluelet.com

FUN FACT

Canada has more than 202,000 kilometres of coastline, more than any other country in the world.

WITNESS
A CARIBOU MIGRATION

Hooves beating on the ground, antlers bobbing across the horizon, calves moving swiftly beside their mothers—these are the sights and sounds you can experience during a caribou migration in Canada. Hundreds of thousands of caribou break off into smaller groups for their journey. They put on an impressive show as they swim through icy lakes, run across the colourful tundra, and coast across the snowy arctic ground. The wilderness surrounding them accentuates the awe of their journey. Their passage occasionally takes pause for mating and male sparring, and other species, such as wolverines, may join them on their way.

Migrations take place in Canada's Arctic, through the Northwest Territories, the Yukon, Nunavut, and in northern Quebec. Migrations happen at various times throughout the year, depending on the migrating herd. You can plan your own excursion in hopes of catching a glimpse of this fascinating trip or book a safari with a reputable tour company.

FUN FACT

Reindeer and caribou are essentially the same animal, but unlike reindeer, the larger caribou has never been domesticated. So you will never see a caribou pulling Santa's sleigh!

CARIBOU AND REINDEER MIGRATION SAFARIS

Arctic Haven Wilderness Lodge
Weber Arctic
Yellowknife, NT X1A 2N9
1-819-923-0932
weberarctic.com

The Great Canadian Adventure Company
52509 Range Rd. 192
Beaver County, AB T0B 4J5
1-780-414-1676
adventures.com

Natural World Safaris
Second Floor Office
130A Western Rd.
Brighton, UK BN1 2LA
+44-1273-691642
naturalworldsafaris.com

Touch the Arctic Tours
5105 Forty-Eighth St.
Yellowknife, NT
X1A 1N5
1-844-606-6784
touchthearctictours.com

5

RIDE
THE ROCKY MOUNTAINEER

Named one of the World's Greatest Trips by *National Geographic*, this iconic luxury train takes you on a journey through Western Canada. The ride offers breathtaking views of the coast, mountains, glaciers, and canyons. Those with a keen eye may catch a glimpse of such wildlife as bears, bald eagles, or bighorn sheep. While you revel in the spectacular views, savour gourmet meals prepared by award-winning chefs. Throughout the trip, passengers have the option to hear stories about the history of the land.

The adventure isn't limited to the time on board the train. Before the sun sets each day, the Rocky Mountaineer comes to a stop and shuttles you to overnight destinations, such as Jasper or Lake Louise. Each stop has opportunities for sightseeing before you settle into a hotel for the night. Your journey on board the Rocky Mountaineer begins again in the morning.

1100-980 Howe St.
Vancouver, BC V6Z 0C8
1-877-460-3200
rockymountaineer.com

FUN FACT

Kicking Horse Pass at the border of Alberta and British Columbia was so steep that the very first locomotive to use it became a runaway train. This happened frequently for more than two decades until the Spiral Tunnels were completed and replaced the pass.

THE FOUR ROCKY MOUNTAINEER ROUTES

The Coastal Package
The only cross-border route with the Rocky Mountaineer, this journey travels between Seattle and Vancouver and through the Rocky Mountains.

The First Passage to the West
See where the last spike from the Canadian Pacific Railway was driven on this route through Vancouver, Kamloops, Lake Louise, and Banff.

Journey through the Clouds
Follow the Fraser River, famous for being home to B.C.'s largest salmon run, and spot the highest peak in the Canadian Rockies while you travel from Vancouver to Kamloops and on to Jasper.

Rain Forest to Gold Rush
From rain forest to desert to mountains, the scenery on this route from Vancouver through Whistler, Quesnel, and Jasper will impress.

ATTEND
THE CALGARY STAMPEDE

A cowboy hat and Western boots are optional but highly recommended when you visit the Calgary Stampede. Dubbed "the greatest outdoor show on earth," the stampede is a ten-day experience that takes place each July. An authentic Western rodeo complete with barrel races, roping, and bull riding is the perfect way to introduce the crowd to Western traditions. It is a highlight for the exhibition, as are the midway and live performances.

The Calgary Stampede has been sharing Western culture and history since 1912. Every year the Siksika, Piikani, Kainai, Tsuut'ina, and Stoney Nakoda First Nations tribes share their heritage, art, and stories here. Agriculture showcases immerse visitors in the rural way of life and allow them to visit a variety of farm animals. As is often the case, however, the food is one of the biggest draws to the stampede. Each year new midway treats are offered along with past favourites.

1410 Olympic Way SE
Calgary, AB T2G 2W1
1-800-661-1767
calgarystampede.com

FUN FACT

Alberta, Canada, is the only region in the world free of Norwegian rats.

7

SLIDE DOWN A WATERSLIDE

IN NORTH AMERICA'S LARGEST SHOPPING MALL

Once the world's largest mall, the West Edmonton Mall is now the largest in North America. Beyond the typical retail stores and food courts, this mall is a vacation experience. Visitors can stay in a pirate-themed hotel room, practice ice skating, and eat at a different venue for every meal. The waterpark is home to waterslides, a wave pool, cabanas, and hot tubs. Little kids can play in the splash pad while the older children learn to surf on a Flowrider.

Families will enjoy a day at the underground aquarium or the indoor amusement park, or spend some quality time bowling or mini golfing. A casino, dinner theatre, and shooting gallery are some of the hot spots for adults visiting the mall. Oh, and if you need some shoes, you can find those there too.

8882 170 St. NW
Edmonton, AB T5T 4J2
1-780-444-5321
wem.ca

FUN FACT

Edmonton is home to the world's tallest streetcar bridge. The High Level Bridge Streetcar was built in 1912.

RIDE
THE AGAWA CANYON TOUR TRAIN

Breathe in Northern Ontario's crisp autumn air while you take a fall ride on the Agawa Canyon Tour Train from Sault Ste. Marie to the Agawa Canyon Wilderness Park. Best seen in late September and early October, these rolling hills of amber and crimson leaves were the inspiration for the Group of Seven's famous artwork. A one-day tour, the Agawa Canyon Tour Train takes you on a 114-mile adventure along shimmering lakes, over two trestles, and on a five-hundred-foot descent into the canyon. Hiking trails and the tour train are the only way to reach the canyon, where train guests are treated to a ninety-minute stopover.

Agawa Canyon Wilderness Park is home to the beautiful Bridal Veil Falls, North and South Black Beaver Falls, and Otter Creek Falls. Follow the trails or climb more than three hundred steps to reach the lookout, where you will take in the true glory of the area.

129 Bay St.
Sault Ste. Marie, ON P6A 6Y2
1-800-461-6020
agawatrain.com

FUN FACT

Sault Ste. Marie, Ontario, and Sault Ste. Marie, Michigan, were one city until the border was established after the War of 1812, dividing the city between two countries.

9

SEARCH
THROUGH NATURAL CAVES AND CAVERNS

At the Blue Mountains, on the highest part of the Niagara escarpment, you will find the Collingwood Scenic Caves, a UNESCO World Heritage Site. These seventeen unique crevices were carved into the rock millions of years ago by glacial ice. They create a labyrinth through the limestone, with each cave named according to its features, such as "Fat Man's Misery," which is a crevice only thirty-six centimetres wide.

Outside of the caves are trails and lookouts that provide outstanding views of Georgian Bay. Daredevils zipline over the treetops and appear to vanish into the forest. A 420-foot-long suspension bridge hovers more than eighty feet above the ground, providing 360-degree views of the area. An autumn visit showcases the colourful forest getting ready to shed leaves for the winter, but there is beauty all year long.

260 Scenic Caves Rd.
Blue Mountains, ON L9Y 0P2
1-705-446-0256
sceniccaves.com

FUN FACT

Georgian Bay is large enough to be considered one of the world's largest lakes, but it isn't a lake.

10

ENTER
QUEBEC'S WALLED CITY

Walking through the stone arches into Old Québec is like stepping back in time. The cobblestone streets are lined with cafés and quaint shops. On a summer day, the air is filled with the sound of buskers sharing their musical talents, while street artists create souvenirs for tourists. Steeples peek out over the trees, and the Saint Lawrence River offers a stunning panorama. Visitors pose for a photo in front of one of the many murals that tell the story of this French-speaking city.

Founded in 1608, Old Québec is now a UNESCO World Heritage Site and the only walled city north of Mexico. Best seen on foot, the fortified city offers many walking and food tours, with a French flair, impressive stone architecture, and a multitude of exceptional places to shop and eat. You will be compelled to visit Old Québec more than once.

quebec-cite.com/en/old-quebec

FUN FACT

Montmorency Falls is just beyond downtown Québec City. These waterfalls are more than eighty metres tall, making them thirty metres higher than Niagara Falls.

THINGS TO SEE IN OLD QUÉBEC

MUSEUMS

Musée de la civilisation
85, rue Dalhousie,
Québec, QC GIK 8R2
1-418-643-2158
mcq.org

Musée du Fort
10, rue Sainte-Anne, C.P.
833, Haute-Ville
Québec, QC G1R 4S7
1-418-692-2175
museedufort.com

Musée national des beaux-arts du Québec
179 Grande Allée Ouest
Québec, QC G1R 2H1
1-418-643-2150
mnbaq.org

LANDMARKS

Château Frontenac (most photographed hotel)
1 rue des Carrières
Québec, QC G1R 4P5
1-418-692-3861
fairmont.com/frontenac-quebec

Citadelle of Québec (National Historic Site)
1 Côte de la Citadelle
Québec, QC G1R 3R2
1-418-694-2815
lacitadelle.qc.ca

Morrin Centre (cultural centre)
44 Chaussée des Écossais
Québec, QC G1R 4H3
1-418-694-9147
morrin.org

Sainte-Anne-de-Beaupré Shrine
10018 avenue Royale
Sainte-Anne-de-Beaupré,
Québec, QC G0A 3C0
1-418-827-3781
sanctuairesainteanne.org

TAKE A NIGHT WALK
IN SEARCH OF A GIANT

Your Tonga Lumina journey begins at the foot of the mountain when a medallion is placed around your neck. The medallion begins to glow as you take the nighttime gondola ride upwards. The smell of the forest and the crunching of the brush add to the mystery as you follow the trail that is magically coming to life with lights and sound.

Tonga Lumina is a night walk in search of the giant through the mountains of Mont-Tremblant, Quebec. As the protector of nature, the giant is waking from his sleep and has a message to share. The guided tour takes you down trails and through nature to clues that will lead you to the giant and all the secrets that he holds. A tale of emergence, the search for the giant is filled with wonder and leaves the explorer feeling a deep connection to nature.

1000 Chemin des Voyageurs
Mont-Tremblant, QC J8E 1T1
1-866-787-8920
tongalumina.ca

FUN FACT

Tremblant, French for "trembling," was named as such because local natives believed there was a great deity who lived inside the mountain, causing it to tremble when he was upset.

SIMILAR NIGHT WALKS IN CANADA

Vallea Lumina
4293 Mountain Square #211, Whistler, BC V8E 1B8
1-833-800-8480
vallealumina.com

Lumina Borealis
1 Fort Henry Dr., Kingston, ON K7K 5G8
1-800-437-2233
luminaborealis.com

Anima Lumina
2230, boulevard du Jardin
Saint-Félicien, QC G8K 0H1
1-418-679-0543
zoosauvage.org/en/anima-lumina

Foresta Lumina
Parc de la Gorge de Coaticook
135, Michaud St., Coaticook, QC J1A 2A4
1-888-524-6743
forestalumina.com

Nova Lumina
75, Chemin de la Plage
Pabos Mills, QC G0C 2J0
1-581-361-0065
bourgdepabos.com

12

SLEEP
IN AN ICE HOTEL

Composed of more than five hundred tonnes of ice and snow, the Hotel de Glace is one of Quebec's most unique hotels. Everything, right down to the art on the walls and the glass you drink from, is made from ice. Local artists create chandeliers, furniture, and ice sculptures for each uniquely themed guest room. Visitors can also try ice carving after taking a tour of the hotel.

Comfort may not be the first thing that comes to mind when you think of an ice hotel, but you might be pleasantly surprised. The ice beds are topped with comfortable mattresses, and guests are provided with thermal sleeping bags designed to withstand the chilly temperatures. Ice walls ensure a quiet night free from the sounds of other guests moving around the hotel, but if the experience is too chilly for you, Hotel de Glace guests are reserved a heated room at a nearby hotel, and they can make the move at any time.

1860, boulevard Valcartier
Saint-Gabriel-de-Valcartier, QC G0A 4S0
1-888-384-5524
valcartier.com

FUN FACT

Twenty miles of tunnels can be found under Montreal. This underground city connects schools, offices, hotels, banks, and malls, helping residents stay warm in the winter and cool in the summer.

OTHER UNIQUE ACCOMMODATIONS IN CANADA

Treehouse Spheres in British Columbia
420 Horne Lake Rd.
Qualicum Beach, BC
V9K 1Z7, 1-250-757-9445
freespiritspheres.com

Caboose in Alberta
Mossleigh, AB T0L 1P0
1-403-534-2129
aspencrossing.com/caboose-cabins

Yurt in Saskatchewan
Emma Lake, SK
1-306-961-9554
florabora.ca

Barn in Manitoba
Russell, MB R0J 1W0
1-204-773-0019
barninthebush.com

Lighthouse in Ontario
Bruce Mines, ON P0R 1C0
1-705-785-3473
brucebaycottages.com

Teepees in Quebec
161 Simon-Ottawa,
Manawan, QC J0K 1M0
1-819-971-1190
voyageamerindiens.com

Stargazer Domes in New Brunswick
86 Old Reach Rd.
Kingston, NB E5N 1B2
1-506-763-2617
ridgebacklodge.com

Rotating Hotel in Prince Edward Island
130 Lantern Hill Dr.
North Rustico, PE C0A 1N0
1-866-557-8383
aroundthesea.ca

Lodge in a Biosphere Reserve in Nova Scotia
189 Trout Point Rd., East
Kemptville, NS B5A 5X9
1-902-761-2142
troutpoint.com

Modern Design and Sustainability in Newfoundland
210 Main Rd., Joe Batt's Arm
NL A0G 2XO, 1-709-658-3444
fogoislandinn.com

13

SAIL
ON THE SAINT LAWRENCE RIVER

Follow the path once sailed by early explorers and sail along the world's longest, widest, and deepest estuary, the Saint Lawrence River and Seaway. Connecting the Great Lakes to the Atlantic Ocean, the river is also part of the international border between Canada and the USA. With some of the best views of the Canadian Shield and a landscape that was carved by glaciers, a scenic river cruise along the Saint Lawrence is breathtaking. Cruises that reach the Gulf of Saint Lawrence make it possible to see whales in their natural habitat and many varieties of birds along the way. Guests are often treated to the unique experience of a seaway lock and learn the history of Canada at the many ports of call in Ontario and Quebec.

FUN FACT

Canada has more lakes than any other country in the world, and 20 percent of the world's fresh water is found in Canada.

RIVER CRUISE COMPANIES

SAINT LAWRENCE RIVER:

CTMA Cruises
435, chemin Avila-Arseneau,
Cap-aux-Meules, QC G4T
1J3 1-418-986-3278
croisieresctma.ca

Rockport Cruises
20 Front St.
Rockport, ON K0E 1V0
1-613-659-3402
rockportcruises.com

Cruise the Saint Lawrence
84, rue St.-Germain Est.,
Ste. 206, Rimouski,
QC G5L 1A6
1-418-725-0135
cruisesaintlawrence.com

Saint Lawrence Cruise Lines
253 Ontario St., Ste. 200
Kingston, ON K7L 2Z4
1-613-549-8091
stlawrencerivercruise.com

OTHER CANADIAN RIVER CRUISES:

Gananoque Boat Line
280 Main St., Gananoque,
ON K7G 2M2
1-613-382-2144
ganboatline.com

Lady Muskoka
300 Ecclestone Dr.
Bracebridge, ON P1L 1G4
1-705-646-2628
ladymuskoka.com

Grand River Dinner Cruises
36 Brant County Rd. 22,
Caledonia, ON N3W 2G9
1-905-765-4107
grandrivercruises.ca

Liftlock and Riverboat Cruises
92 George St. N.
Peterborough, ON K9J 3G6
1-705-742-9912
liftlockcruises.com

Ontario Waterway Cruises
Orillia, ON L3V 6H9
1-800-561-5767
ontariowaterwaycruises.com

14

GET A BIRD'S-EYE VIEW
OF NOVA SCOTIA

The fresh early morning air, the cool breeze, and the gentle floating of the balloon make flying in a hot air balloon a surprisingly relaxing experience. The occasional interruption of the roar from the burners ensures you stay afloat while taking in a view like no other.

Flying over the Annapolis Valley in Nova Scotia in a hot air balloon is an incredible way to grasp the beauty of this maritime province. The ground below shifts from treetops to a landscape checkered with farmers' fields and dotted with lakes. Soon the vineyards appear, and the rivers snake across the land. The stunning Bay of Fundy is on the horizon.

No two hot air balloon rides are the same, as the wind dictates some of the trip, but they all end with a celebratory glass of champagne.

East Coast Balloon Adventures
New Minas, Bay of Fundy, and Annapolis Valley
1-902-306-0095
eastcoastballoonadventures.com

FUN FACT

Halifax, Nova Scotia, is home to the Maritime Museum of the Atlantic, the oldest and largest maritime museum in Canada.

ENCOUNTER WILD HORSES
ON SABLE ISLAND

Three hundred kilometres southeast of Halifax sits a tiny, narrow sandbar known as Sable Island. This remote island is one of the farthest offshore islands in Canada and can be reached only by sea or air after registering your visit with Parks Canada. The journey is worth it when you arrive on the sandy island beaches and see the hoofprints of hundreds of Sable horses in the sand.

Sable Island is home to approximately five hundred of these feral horses, whose ancestors were abandoned in the eighteenth century. They have no specific breed of their own, as they are mixed with many breeds of horses, but they are most often small horses and dark in colour. They can be seen grazing in the tall grass, trotting along the beach, posing for photos, and even showing curiosity towards tourists on the island.

pc.gc.ca/en/pn np/ns/sable

FUN FACT

Sable Island is home to the world's biggest breeding colony of grey seals.

16

GET SCREECHED
IN NEWFOUNDLAND

All "come from aways" (that's Newfoundlander for tourist) visiting this eastern province can get screeched in a local pub. The "screech-in" is a rite of passage for tourists to embrace the culture, form bonds with the locals, and be named an official Newfoundlander. Newfoundland Screech is 40 percent rum, but a screech-in may involve any strong alcohol. The ritual varies from place to place, with a ceremony leader guiding the screech-in with hearty cheers from the crowd. The participant will introduce themselves, respond to questions from the leader, drink a shot of screech, and kiss a cod. Once the custom has been performed, the come from away is named an official Newfoundlander by the ceremony leader. On occasion, the participant will need to eat a piece of Newfie steak before being declared an official Newfoundlander, but don't worry. It's just bologna.

FUN FACT

Newfoundland is the foggiest place in the world, with more than two hundred days of fog each year.

BE AMAZED
BY THE BAY OF FUNDY

The Bay of Fundy is an anomaly. It has the world's highest tides, so you wouldn't expect to see the ocean floor within the same day, but that is exactly what happens twice a day at this stunning bay. Visitors can kayak on the high tides and then walk on the sand that was beneath their kayak just hours before. It takes just over six hours for the tides to shift, so spending a day in the area will give you a chance to get the full experience. While there, take in the allure of the Hopewell Rocks. In high tide, the rocks resemble huge flowerpots, with the trees sitting on top. When the tide goes out, the narrow base of each rock is exposed, providing a new perspective. Walk to the base of the rocks to realize how massive they are.

In between the high and low tide, take a whale-watching tour or go in search of one of the nine hundred pairs of breeding Atlantic puffins that live in the area.

bayoffundytourism.com

FUN FACT

Not far from the Bay of Fundy is the Old Sow Whirlpool, which is the second-largest whirlpool in the world.

DANCE
AT A MUSIC FESTIVAL

Music has charms to soothe the savage beast, and a music festival captivates the souls of thousands. There is something deeply connective about gathering with your friends and hundreds of potential friends to celebrate your shared love for music. There is excitement to hear bands you love and discover new music groups. The collective pulse of the crowd swaying to the music creates camaraderie while you become a part of history.

Canadians host music festivals that celebrate art and music across the country. They vary from folk music to jazz festivals and every other genre. There are multiday festivals with camping right on site, single-day festivals, and multiday festivals without camping. Musicians and other artists share their inspiring talents at these musical celebrations.

FUN FACT

Some of Canada's most successful musicians include Neil Young, Avril Lavigne, Paul Anka, Celine Dion, and Justin Bieber.

SOME MUSIC FESTIVALS IN CANADA

Shambhala Music Festival
Salmo River Ranch, BC
shambhalamusicfestival.com

Big Valley Jamboree
Camrose, AB
bigvalleyjamboree.com

Regina Folk Festival
Regina, SK
reginafolkfestival.com

Dauphin's Countryfest
Dauphin, MB
countryfest.ca

Boots and Hearts
Oro-Medonte, ON
bootsandhearts.com

Harvest Jazz & Blues Festival
Fredericton, NB
harvestjazzandblues.com

Halifax Jazz Festival
Halifax, NS
halifaxjazzfestival.ca

Cavendish Beach Music Festival
Cavendish, PEI
cavendishbeachmusic.com

George Street Festival
St. John's, NL
georgestreetlive.ca

Festival International de Jazz de Montréal
Montreal, QC
montrealjazzfest.com

BEHOLD
THE RCMP MUSICAL RIDE

Adorned in the traditional red serge, blue riding pants with a yellow stripe, riding boots, and campaign hat, the Royal Canadian Mounted Police (RCMP) share the heritage of the police force in the RCMP Musical Ride. The musical ride is a touring cavalry that displays its equestrian skills on the backs of thoroughbred horses. Each of the thirty-two riders is a member of the RCMP, Canada's federal police force.

The RCMP Musical Ride began in 1887 and continues today around the world. The purpose of the tour is promotion of the RCMP and their heritage. While the RCMP no longer officially use horses in their day-to-day business, it was once an important part of the operation. Witnessing these respected officers sitting proudly on their horses and holding their flags is a truly proud Canadian moment.

rcmp-grc.gc.ca/even/en/t/2/e

FUN FACT

Intrepid Park, Ontario, was once home to Camp X, a spy school during World War II. The school became a spy interception station after the war until it closed in 1969.

WITNESS
THE MONARCH BUTTERFLY MIGRATION

Monarch butterflies, with their deep-orange wings, are a common sight in Ontario, but for a few days each fall they put on a display at Point Pelee that is anything but common.

Point Pelee is the southernmost tip of mainland Canada. The land narrows into a "V" pointing at Lake Erie and towards the United States. This funnel is the starting point to the shortest distance from Canada to Mexico. This, along with the presence of milkweed in the area, is believed to be the reason for the monarch butterfly migration from Point Pelee each fall. Thousands of butterflies flock to the point before making the three-thousand-kilometre trip to Central Mexico.

pelee.com/monarch-butterfly-migration

FUN FACT

Point Pelee is also a popular stop for migrating birds, including many rare species and songbirds.

FOOD AND DRINK

BITE
INTO SOME BANNOCK

Bannock is a simple fried bread made of flour, baking powder, milk, and oil that is a popular comfort food in Nunavut. It was brought to the territory by Scottish fur traders, and the simplicity and long shelf life of bannock was appreciated by the First Nations. Because it is quick to make and travels well, it remains a staple today. Originally, the Scottish made their bread on a bannock stone that was placed on the floor in front of a fire. Today, it is made in the oven or fryer, and some campers still make it over an open fire. There are virtually thousands of recipes for bannock that include various spices, berries, raisins, and other ingredients. It can be eaten alone or served alongside any meal.

FUN FACT

Game meat, including reindeer, moose, and caribou, were staples in the First Nations people's diets and are still popular in Northern Canada.

INDULGE
IN A NANAIMO BAR

Named after the city of Nanaimo in British Columbia, Nanaimo bars are sweet dessert squares that originated in Canada and are enjoyed across the country. These tasty treats consist of a crumbly chocolate and coconut base covered in a rich and creamy custard icing and topped with a thin layer of hard chocolate ganache. The three different textures and layers of sweetness make each bite of the Nanaimo bar one to be celebrated.

Alternatives to the original custard Nanaimo bar include innovative flavors, such as mint, cherry, cappuccino, peanut butter, Grand Marnier, and Baileys Irish cream filling. For the tastiest of all the Nanaimo bars, seek out bakeries and restaurants across Canada that can treat you to a freshly made bar.

FUN FACT

Nanaimo, British Columbia, is also known for its annual bathtub races.

ENJOY A SLICE
OF SASKATOON BERRY PIE

At first glance, one might think that a saskatoon berry is a blueberry, but their similarities are only visual. These sweet and nutty berries are part of the apple family, and some describe the flavour as a combination of grapes, cherries, and almonds. They make the most delicious pie when you combine them with sugar and butter and bake them in a flaky pastry crust. While many recipes call for lemon zest, omitting this ingredient is the secret to a bolder berry flavour. Eat your saskatoon berry pie warm with a scoop of vanilla ice cream on top and you will be a devoted fan for life.

Contrary to popular belief, the Saskatoon berry is not named after Saskatoon, Saskatchewan. The city is named after the berry, from the Cree word for the berries, "mis-sask-quah-too-mina." It is also called a prairie berry.

FUN FACT

In Saskatchewan, a hoodie is called a "bunnyhug."

TOUR
TORONTO'S DISTILLERY DISTRICT

The Gooderham and Worts distillery was founded in 1832 and by the late 1860s was the largest distillery in the world. Today, it is the backdrop for Toronto's Distillery District. This National Historic Site is a pedestrian village packed full of culinary treats and spirits. Not coincidentally, Mill Street Brewery is located on Mill Street in the district and is just one of the craft breweries you can visit on a tour. There are art galleries, shops, a noodle bar, an oyster house, a sake bar, ice cream shops, and fine dining. It is truly a one-stop shop for foodies.

Toronto's Distillery District is home to the famous Christmas market it holds every year. With the scent of hot apple cider in the air, twinkling Christmas lights, and carols playing, it puts everyone in the holiday spirit.

9 Trinity St., Ste. 200
Toronto, ON M5A 3C4
1-416-364-1177
thedistillerydistrict.com

FUN FACT

Legends say that the ghost of James Worts, one of the founders of Gooderham and Worts, appeared after his early and tragic death and continues to haunt the Distillery District today.

CHASE
THE CHEESE TRAIL

The Oxford County Cheese Trail is a journey through some of Ontario's small towns and rural communities with a focus on locally sourced dairy and cheese. The self-guided tour leads you to farmers' markets, restaurants, and bakeries, where you tempt your taste buds with fresh dairy products and a variety of delicious cheeses. Find artisanal cheese in local cheese shops and discover delicious baked goods and cheese platters at retail stores and cafés. This tour has stops at museums, where you can learn how to churn butter and discover the agricultural history of the area. Spread the tour over a couple of days and grab the opportunity to spend the night at the Elm Hurst Inn & Spa.

oxfordcountycheesetrail.ca

FUN FACT

One of Canada's most exported cheeses, Oka, was originally made by monks and is still made today in Oka, Quebec.

GRAB A BAGEL
IN MONTREAL

New York may be the first place you think of when bagels are mentioned, but Montreal has a bagel empire like no other. Montreal bagels are handmade, small, and dense, with a larger hole than other bagels. Their sweet flavour and chewiness comes from being boiled in honey water before they are baked in a wood-fired oven. The result is a perfectly golden bagel best enjoyed warm and plain.

St-Viateur Bagel began preparing genuine Montreal bagels in 1957. It still bakes these delicious bagels today in what is known as the longest-running bagel shop in Montreal. Montreal native and astronaut Gregory Chamitoff loves his bagels from Fairmount Bagel so much that he took three bags of them to the International Space Station.

St-Viateur Bagel Shop
263, Rue St-Viateur O.
Montreal, Quebec, H2V 1Y1
514-276-8044/
stviateurbagel.com

Fairmount Bagel
74 Fairmount Ouest Ave.
Montreal, Quebec, H2T 2M2
514.272.0667
fairmountbagel.com

FUN FACT

Montreal has the greatest number of restaurants per capita in all of Canada.

HAVE
AN AUTHENTIC NOVA SCOTIAN LOBSTER ROLL

The Nova Scotian lobster roll combines luxury cuisine with a simple white roll, much like a hot dog bun. This brilliant combination was invented by fishermen in the 1890s who needed a way to sell extra lobster meat to people passing by the docks. The delicate and flaky lobster meat doesn't travel well without a vessel, so the buns were used, and the lobster roll was born. The most common lobster rolls are made with a combination of lobster, mayonnaise, and lemon juice on a white bun, but many street food vendors and restaurants have elevated their lobster rolls, using artisanal buns and adding special ingredients, such as bacon or avocado. You will find lobster rolls everywhere in the maritime provinces, even on the McDonald's menu in the summer months.

FUN FACT

Nova Scotia has strong Scottish ties and the province's name is latin for "New Scotland."

28

FOLLOW
THE GOOD CHEER TRAIL

Hospitality, local brews, new discoveries, and the potential to win prizes are what make the Good Cheer Trail special. It is Canada's first and only tour that is a combination of vineyards, pubs, craft breweries, cideries, and distilleries. More than fifty locations across Nova Scotia participate in this spirited trail, sharing their locally produced beverages with eager customers. More than just a fun tour, the Good Cheer Trail gives everyone a passport to get stamped after uploading a photo at each participating stop on the trail. Every ten stamps earn you an entry into a grand prize draw, and fifteen stamps get you a free Good Cheer Trail T-shirt.

goodcheertrail.com

FUN FACT

Nova Scotia is also home to the Lobster Trail (novascotialobstertrail.com) and Chowder Trail (novascotiachowdertrail.com).

DELIGHT YOUR TASTE BUDS WITH BEAVERTAILS

Also known as the Canadian doughnut, this national treat was once called keekla but gained the name "beaver tail" because of the flat, oblong shape, like that of a beaver's tail. This makes it the most Canadian dessert ever, because the beaver is a Canadian emblem. Eventually, the name BeaverTails was capitalized on and remains a popular restaurant today.

The original recipe is a flat deep-fried dough that is covered in a cinnamon and sugar coating. These days you will find many variations on the original recipe with such toppings as whipped cream, bananas, berries, Nutella, and chocolate. Most of these are found at the BeaverTails restaurants and stands in Canada. Even President Obama treated himself to one on a Canadian visit.

beavertails.com

FUN FACT

The beaver is a Canadian emblem that predates the maple leaf. Originating from the importance of beaver pelts in the fur trade, the Hudson Bay Company put the beaver on its coat of arms in 1678. It is found on the Canadian nickel today.

EAT YOUR WAY
THROUGH A FOOD FESTIVAL

A food festival is a gathering with tables of delicious treats, a legion of scents in the air, and satiated people all around. These festivals are the best places to discover new cuisine, get adventurous with your taste buds, and be awed by the culinary artistry of the chefs. The food is the main event, but most food festivals offer a well-rounded mixture of art and music along with the food, keeping entire families entertained. Each festival has a unique theme, such as street food, wine, or even poutine. Most vendors and chefs use locally sourced ingredients in their recipes, so the community gets the full benefit of the festival, and visitors get the freshest and most delicious fare.

FUN FACT

Canadian bacon, also known as peameal bacon, is often mistaken for ham. It is a cured pork loin rolled in crushed yellow peas.

FOOD FESTIVALS

BC Seafood Festival
1-250-400-2882
bcseafoodfestival.com

The Great Canadian Beer Festival
1-250-590-7663
victoriabeersociety.com

Vancouver International Wine Festival
1-877-321-3121
vanwinefest.ca

Taste of Edmonton
1-780-423-2822
tasteofedm.ca

Taste of Saskatchewan
1-306-975-3175
tasteofsaskatchewan.ca

Morden Corn & Apple Festival
cornandapple.com

Apple Pie Trail Ciderfest
1-705-444-7398
applepietrail.com

Canada's Largest Ribfest
canadaslargestribfest.com

Taste of the Danforth
1-416-469-5634
tasteofthedanforth.com

Festival de la Poutine
1-819-967-1423
festivaldelapoutine.com

Taste of the Caribbean
totc.ca

Prince Edward Island International Shellfish Festival
1-866-955-2003
peishellfish.com

Shediac Lobster Festival
1-506-532-1122
shediaclobsterfestival.ca

31

SATISFY YOUR SWEET TOOTH WITH A BUTTER TART

Visitors to Canada should not return home without first savouring a butter tart. A small pastry with a gooey center and crunchy top, the butter tart is one of Canada's proudest culinary creations. The thick and flaky crust of the tart shell shares equal billing with the deliciously rich mixture it contains. Together, they provide a combination of melt-in-your-mouth pastry and a delightful sweetness that will make your taste buds tingle.

Although there are several ways to make a butter tart, the ingredients primarily consist of butter, sugar, syrup, and eggs. The country is divided on whether raisins, walnuts, or pecans belong inside a butter tart, but they all agree that this is one of their most delectable treats.

FUN FACT

Another popular dish invented by a Canadian is the Hawaiian pizza: a pizza topped with ham, pineapple, and extra cheese.

BUTTER TART FESTIVALS

Ontario's Best Butter Tart Festival
1-705-526-4275
buttertartfestival.ca

Kawarthas Northumberland Butter Tart Tour
self-guided tour to more than fifty locations
buttertarttour.ca

Muskoka Butter Tart Festival
1-705-765-5367
mlmuseum.com/special-events

The Queensway Butter Tart Festival
1-416-684-7137
shopthequeensway.com/tartfestival

The Great Canadian ButterTart Festival
1-519-442 6324 ext. 3209

SAVOUR
A PLATE OF POUTINE

Pronounced “poo-teen” in much of Canada and “poo-tin” in Quebec, where it originated, this savoury dish consists of thick, deep-fried french fries covered in white cheddar cheese curds that begin to melt when they are topped with a hot brown gravy. Appropriately, the word “poutine” is slang for “messy” in Quebec.

A source of pride for Quebec, poutine is found in abundance in the French province, and it is also readily available at restaurants and food trucks throughout the country. The popularity of the dish has compelled chefs to create variations, such as pulled pork poutine, bacon poutine, and poutine pizza. Whichever creation you choose, remember that the secret lies in the cheese. Never settle for anything less than authentic cheese curds if you want the true poutine experience.

FUN FACT

The original poutine recipe was just french fries and cheese curds. Gravy was added many years later, and it became the poutine we know today.

TRY POUTINE FROM ONE OF THESE RESTAURANTS

Belgian Fries
1885 Commercial Dr.
Vancouver, BC V5N 4A6
1-604-253-4220
belgianfries.ca

Boomers Gourmet Fries
26 Erie St.
Stratford, ON N5A 1B2
1-519-275-3147
boomersgourmetfries.ca

La Banquise
994, rue Rachel Est
Montréal, QC H2J 2J3
1-514-525-2415
labanquise.com

Restaurant Le Roy Jucep
1050, boul. Saint-Joseph
Drummondville, QC J2C 2C6
1-819-478-4848
jucep.com

Poutineville
many locations throughout Québec, including
1365 Ontario Est
Montréal, QC H2L 1S1
1-514-419-5444
poutineville.com

DRINK A CAESAR

The Caesar is Canada's official cocktail. This spicy yet refreshing drink originated in Calgary when a wise bartender decided to add clam juice to the traditional Bloody Mary and named it the Bloody Caesar. Rather than squeezing clam juice into tomato juice, today the Caesar is made using Clamato juice, Worcestershire sauce, tabasco sauce, and vodka. A little celery salt around the rim and a celery stick in the glass finish the drink off nicely. With more than 350 million Caesars being made each year, it is obviously a popular drink for Canadians. You can find it in almost every bar and licensed restaurant across the country, or you can buy canned Caesars at Canadian liquor stores.

FUN FACT

Another twist on the Bloody Mary is the Bloody Lobster, which adds lobster juice to the drink.

TRY MAPLE SYRUP
ON A STICK

There is no substitute for the naturally sweet and smooth flavour of pure maple syrup. It is the most delectable topping when served warm over pancakes or waffles. Maple syrup is used for many sweet treats, such as cotton candy and fudge, but did you know that you can also eat pure maple syrup on a stick? Some people call it maple syrup taffy, while others say it is called snow candy. Whatever you call it, it's a winter tradition in Quebec, and it is very easy to make. Simply gather some clean snow and flatten it onto a baking sheet, boil your maple syrup using a candy thermometer to reach the correct temperature, and pour a line of it onto the fresh snow. Roll a popsicle stick or spoon over the taffy and enjoy your maple syrup like a lollipop.

FUN FACT

Quebec produces more than 75 percent of the world's supply of maple syrup.

MAPLE SYRUP CELEBRATIONS

Elmira Maple Syrup Festival
1-519-669-6000
elmiramaplesyrup.com

Muskoka Maple Trail
1-705-789-4771
muskokamaple.ca

Sugarbush Maple Syrup Festival
1-416-661-6600
maplesyrupfest.com

Sweetwater Harvest Festival
1-705-526-7809
wyemarsh.com/sweetwater

Sucrerie de la Montagne
1-450-451-0831
sucreriedelamontagne.com

Sugar Moon Farm
1-902-657-3348
sugarmoon.ca

APPRECIATE
A GLASS OF CANADIAN WINE

Canada has a unique position in the wine community. While most countries have a specialty wine that they produce very well, the varying climates and geography across Canada make it easy for the country to create many different types of wine. Ontario has the longest growing season in the country, which explains why three-quarters of Canada's grapes are grown in the Niagara Region, but the Okanagan Valley of British Columbia, Pelee Island, Montreal, and Nova Scotia's Annapolis Valley are all known for their full-bodied, fresh, and artisanal red and white wines.

If Canada's first serious step into the world of wine came when Inniskillin ice wine won a prestigious wine award in France. Inniskillin continues to be an award-winning brand today. If Canada had to have a specialty wine, it would be ice wine.

FUN FACT

Ogopogo is a mythical monster that supposedly lives in Lake Okanagan, British Columbia.

FAMOUS CANADIAN WINERIES

Château des Charmes
1025 York Rd.
Niagara-on-the-Lake, ON
L0S 1P0
1-905-262-4219
fromtheboscfamily.com/
chateau-des-charmes

Fielding Winery
4020 Locust Ln.
Beamsville, ON L0R 1B2
1-888-778-7758
fieldingwines.com

Mission Hill Family Estate
1730 Mission Hill Rd.
West Kelowna,
Okanagan Valley
BC, V4T 2E4
1-250-768-6400
missionhillwinery.com

Nichol Vineyard
1285 Smethurst Rd.
Naramata, BC V0H 1N1
1-250-496-5962
nicholvineyard.com

Peller Estates Winery
290 John St. E.
Niagara-on-the-Lake,
ON L0S 1J0
1-888-673-5537
peller.com

Reif Estate Winery
15608 Niagara Pkwy.
Niagara-on-the Lake,
ON L0S 1J0
1-905-468-7738
reifwinery.com

SPORTS AND RECREATION

KAYAK
WITH ORCAS

Orcas, also known as killer whales, are found in the waters around British Columbia. They travel in pods and primarily feed on chinook salmon. People with nerves of steel can kayak amongst them. For the best chance of finding orcas, kayak with a guide and keep your eyes on the horizon. Whalewatching boats are your best indicator that whales are nearby, but you can also watch for fins, flukes, the spray from blowholes, and the print that a whale leaves on the water. This print is a completely smooth glass-like oval where the whale or its fluke has surfaced.

Being in a kayak surrounded by whales is an exhilarating experience. The true size of these ocean predators becomes clear when you are faced with them on the ocean. The sound of the water spraying from the blowhole and the sight of a breaching whale just feet away will invigorate even the most steadfast of people.

FUN FACT

Despite being called "killer whales," orcas are part of the dolphin family.

ORCA KAYAK TOURS

Sea Kayak Adventures
Port McNeill, BC
1-800-616-1943
seakayakadventures.com

Kingfisher Wilderness Adventures Ltd.
Port McNeill, BC
1-866-546-4347
kingfisher.ca

Ecosummer Expeditions
Port McNeill, BC
1-250-674-0102
ecosummer.com

Spirit of the West Adventures
Heriot Bay, BC
1-800-307-3982
kayakingtours.com

North Island Kayak
Telegraph Cove
Vancouver Island, BC
1-250-928-3114
kayakbc.ca

Wildcoast
Quathiaski Cove, Quadra Island, BC
1-855-485-9453
kayakbritishcolumbia.com

SNORKEL
WITH SALMON

The crystal-clear Campbell River on Vancouver Island is where you can find hundreds of thousands of salmon in the summer and fall. In late July, the pink salmon start their run, followed by the chinook, coho, and sockeye salmon in August and September. Chum salmon complete the run in the fall, making this a migration point for all five types of Pacific salmon and the ideal place for you to get in the water with them.

A wetsuit and snorkeling gear are all you need to come face-to-face with some of the largest salmon you can find. This unique experience takes you on the migration journey to their spawning grounds. You could also encounter trout, beavers, seals, and other wildlife in the water or deer and bears on the shore.

Destiny River Adventures
1995 Island Hwy.
Campbell River, BC V9W 2G3
1-877-923-7238
destinyriver.com/snorkel-salmon-adventures

FUN FACT

Salmon are born in fresh water, migrate to the ocean, and then swim upstream back to their birthplace to spawn.

OTHER UNIQUE SNORKELING EXPERIENCES

SNORKEL WITH BELUGA WHALES

Big Fish Expeditions Inc.
Station Central
Victoria, BC V8W 3S3
1-250-588-8267
bigfishexpeditions.com

Churchill Wild
Ile des Chenes, Manitoba Office
Suite 204 – 1 Rivard St.
Ile des Chenes, MB R0A 0T0
1-866-UGO-WILD (846-9453)
churchillwild.com

SNORKEL WITH SEALS

Ocean Trails Resort
1135 Resort Dr.
Parksville, BC V9P 2T6
1-888-248-6212
ocean-trails.com

Sea Dragon Charters
6373 Bruce St.
West Vancouver, BC V7W 2G5
1-855-732-3724
seadragoncharters.com

Sundown Diving
22 Esplanade Rd.
Nanaimo, BC V9R 4Y7
1-250-753-1880
sundowndiving.com

CANOPY WALK
ON A SUSPENSION BRIDGE

Take a walk 230 feet above a rushing river on the Capilano Suspension Bridge. The sound of the water moving below as the wind gently sways the bridge will both soothe and excite you. The 450-foot-long bridge hovers over the rain forest and leads to viewing stations where you can take in the ecosystem around you.

The bridge is the oldest visitor attraction in the area. Adults and children alike can enjoy this nature walk, which is even more beautiful when lit up during the winter holidays. A series of smaller suspension bridges takes you on a canopy walk through the rain forest. Explore the area, discover totem poles, and meet some interesting wildlife.

3735 Capilano Rd.
North Vancouver, BC V7R 4J1
1-604-985-7474
capbridge.com

FUN FACT
The Capilano Suspension Bridge can withstand the weight of ninety-seven elephants.

DIG
FOR DINOSAUR BONES

Dinosaur bones are a common sight at Dinosaur Provincial Park in Brooks, Alberta. Upon arrival, a park guide may even say, "If you throw your hat and don't find a dinosaur bone, you're doing something wrong." This UNESCO World Heritage Site is the final resting place for dinosaurs that roamed the earth more than seventy-five million years ago, and visitors are welcome to explore the area.

Hiking amongst these ancient bones is extraordinary, and more adventurous explorers can sign up for a dinosaur dig expedition, where they journey into the badlands to dig through dirt and rocks that no human has ever touched before. A Paleontologist guide, a small tool kit, and patience is all that is needed for this amazing opportunity where you could make the next big discovery.

albertaparks.ca/parks/south/dinosaur-pp

FUN FACT

Drumheller, Alberta, has the world's largest collection of complete dinosaur skeletons.

GO ICE FISHING
AT LAKE DIEFENBAKER

Tread carefully across the thick ice lake and choose a spot to go ice fishing. For some this means sitting on a chair in the open air, others use a pop-up shelter, and on the high end there are permanent shelters with amenities. The one thing they all have in common is a hole in the ice. Using an ice saw or auger, ice fishermen carve out their fishing hole and set up their fishing lines, rods, or even spears to catch their trophy fish.

Lake Diefenbaker in Saskatchewan is an ideal spot to ice fish for pike, walleye, burbot, or perch. The lake is recognized for its generous bounty, and those who set up their ice shanties there are rarely disappointed. This 225-kilometre lake is 133 kilometres south of Saskatoon.

FUN FACT

Saskatchewan has more roads than any other Canadian province.

JOIN
A POLAR BEAR EXPEDITION

There is nothing quite as majestic and fear inducing as a polar bear in the wild. These lords of the Arctic can grow to be more than one thousand pounds. Their imposing size should be feared because they have no natural predators and are not easily intimidated. For these reasons, polar bears are not often viewed in the wild, making the Churchill experience extraordinary.

Nature enthusiasts can safely watch polar bears in their natural environment on a guided tour in Churchill, Manitoba. In October and November of each year, the white giants cross the subarctic tundra to reach their seal hunting ground in the Hudson Bay. From the warmth and safety of a lodge or tundra vehicle, you can watch them make their journey across the snow.

everythingchurchill.com/experiences/polar-bears

FUN FACT

Many Churchill residents leave their car doors unlocked to offer a safe space for anyone who encounters a polar bear.

SKATE
ON THE RED RIVER MUTUAL TRAIL

Abandon the traditional ice-skating routine of skating laps around a rink and head to the world's longest skating rink. The Red River Mutual Trail is found in Winnipeg, Manitoba, and forms every winter when the Red and Assiniboine rivers freeze, providing more than 8.5 kilometres of skating trail. The trail holds the Guinness World Record for the world's longest naturally frozen skating trail.

Winnipeg maintains the trail for optimal use, and people are welcome to skate, walk, run, or slide along the trail. Stop to view sculptures and other art displays along the way, listen to musical performances, or grab a bite to eat before continuing along the trail.

1 Forks Market Rd.
Winnipeg, MB R3C 4L9
1-204-942-6100
theforks.com/events/skating-trail-and-park-conditions

FUN FACT
The world's largest collection of contemporary Inuit art is found at the Winnipeg Art Gallery.

OTHER CANADIAN SKATING TRAILS

Shipyards Skating Loop
Yukon River and
Second Ave.
Whitehorse, YT
1-867-668-8325
whitehorse.ca/shipyardspark

Victoria Park IceWay
12030 River Valley Rd.
Edmonton, AB
T5K 1L4
1-780-442-5311
edmonton.ca/activities_parks_recreation/outdoor-ice-rinks.aspx

Ice Skating Trail at Arrowhead Provincial Park
451 Arrowhead Park Rd.
Huntsville, ON P1H 2J4
1-705-789-5105 ext. 224
discovermuskoka.ca/ice-skating-trail-arrowhead

Rideau Canal Skateway
The skating trail runs from downtown to the Hartwells Locks.
Ottawa, ON
1-800-465-1867
ncc-ccn.gc.ca/rideau-canal-skateway

RiverOak Skating Trail
2900 York's Corners Rd.
Ottawa, ON K0A 2P0
1-613-212-0077
riveroak.ca/skatingtrail

Lac des Loups
9 Montée Beausoleil
Quebec, J0X 3K0
1-819-456 3283
patinageenforet.com

DO THE EDGE WALK
AT THE CN TOWER

The Edge Walk at Toronto's CN Tower is an adventure for the fearless. Step onto a five-foot ledge 116 stories above the ground and walk a full circle around the CN Tower. This is the world's highest hands-free full circle external walk on a building, and while it sounds scary, it is actually quite safe. A guide and a safety harness ensure you remain on the ledge, while the sight of the lake and city below gets your heart rate going. Once your outdoor adventure is done, the CN Tower has more excitement inside. Stand on the glass floor for another vantage point of the streets below and enjoy a meal in the 360-degree rotating restaurant.

290 Bremner Blvd., Toronto, ON M5V 3L9
1-416-868-6937
cntower.ca

FUN FACT

The PATH, a thirty-kilometre walkway under downtown Toronto, is the largest underground shopping mall in North America.

OTHER AREA ATTRACTIONS

Art Gallery of Ontario
317 Dundas St. W.
Toronto, ON M5T 1G4
1-877-225-4246
ago.ca

Bata Shoe Museum
327 Bloor St. W.
Toronto, ON M5S 1W7
1-416-979-7799
batashoemuseum.ca

Hockey Hall of Fame
30 Yonge St.
Toronto, ON M5E 1X8
1-416-360-7765
hhof.com

Ontario Place
955 Lake Shore Blvd. W.
Toronto, ON M6K 3B9
1-416-314-9900
ontarioplace.com

Ripley's Aquarium of Canada
288 Bremner Blvd.
Toronto, ON M5V 3L9
1-647-351-3474
ripleyaquariums.com/Canada

Royal Ontario Museum
100 Queens Park
Toronto, ON M5S 2C6
1-416-586-8000
rom.on.ca

44

WATCH A BALL GAME
UNDER A RETRACTABLE DOME

Originally called the SkyDome but now named the Rogers Centre, this multipurpose stadium was the first in the world to have a fully retractable roof. The dome has a four-paneled retractable roof that sits 282 feet above the ground at its highest point. While retractable roofs are not that uncommon in stadiums these days, it is still unique because it is one of the few multipurpose stadiums, meaning it is used for baseball, football, concerts, and other gatherings.

Toronto's beloved Blue Jays play their home games at the Rogers Centre. On a sunny day, the roof is open, and the CN Tower appears to be looking down over the stadium. It can close in just twenty minutes and protect everyone from the elements. Hotel guests who are lucky enough to have one of the seventy rooms that overlook the field can watch the game from the comfort of their hotel rooms.

Rogers Centre
1 Blue Jays Way
Toronto, ON M5V 1J1
mlb.com/bluejays/ballpark

FUN FACT

Until 1999, Yonge Street in Toronto was mistakenly listed in the Guinness Book of World Records as the longest street in the world at 1,896 kilometres long. It is actually fifty-six kilometres long but runs into Highway 11, which caused the confusion.

HIKE
THE BRUCE PENINSULA

Hear the birds singing overhead, the tinkling of tiny rocks falling down the escarpment, water hitting the shore on Georgian Bay, and the wind rustling through the leaves around you. These are the sounds of the Bruce Trail, Canada's oldest and longest foot trail.

With 890 kilometres of hiking trails through the Bruce Peninsula, you could easily spend a week or more discovering new streams, limestone cliffs, and beautiful beaches along the bay. The trail lookouts provide a spot for contemplating nature's gifts and the ideal opportunity for photographing the aquamarine waters of Georgian Bay. Picnic spots and beaches present an excuse to take a rest. Flowerpot rock formations and the occasional bald eagle flying above will entice hikers to stay longer in search of more natural treasures.

explorethebruce.com/things-to-do/bruce-trail

FUN FACT

A popular swimming spot in Bruce Peninsula National Park is the Grotto, a cave on the shore that was sculpted by the waves hitting the rock.

46

BREAK OUT
OF THE WORLD'S LARGEST ESCAPE ROOM

The Diefenbunker was once a military station built to protect John Diefenbaker, the prime minister at the time, and other important military figures in the event of a nuclear war. Today, the Diefenbunker is a museum in Ottawa and home to the world's largest escape room, "Escape the Diefenbunker."

The escape room runs on weekends and takes up an entire floor of the underground bunker. Your adventure begins with the discovery that the museum is a cover for an enemy spy organization that is planning an attack. You must stop the imminent attack and warn the world, and then escape the Diefenbunker. With just sixty minutes to save the world and make your escape, this is an urgent mission that only you and eleven friends can take on.

3929 Carp Rd.
Carp, ON K0A 1L0
1-613-839-0007
diefenbunker.ca/worlds-largest-escape-room

FUN FACT
The HI Ottawa Jail Hostel is an old jail that was made into a hostel where guests can sleep in solitary confinement.

OTHER OTTAWA-AREA MUSEUMS

Canadian Museum of History
100 Laurier St.
Gatineau, QC K1A 0M8
1-800-555-5621
historymuseum.ca

National Gallery of Canada
380 Sussex Dr.
Ottawa, ON K1N 9N4
1-613-990-1985
gallery.ca

Canadian War Museum
1 Vimy Place
Ottawa, ON K1A 0M8
1-800-555-5621
warmuseum.ca

Canada Science and Technology Museum
1867 St. Laurent Blvd.
Ottawa, ON K1G 5A3
1-866-442-4416
ingeniumcanada.org/cstm

Canada Aviation and Space Museum
11 Aviation Pkwy.
Ottawa, ON K1K 2X5
1-866-442-4416
ingeniumcanada.org/casm

Canada Agriculture and Food Museum
901 Prince of Wales Dr.
Ottawa, ON K1G 5A3
1-866-442-4416
ingeniumcanada.org/cafm

Canadian Museum of Nature
240 McLeod St.
Ottawa, ON K2P 2R1
1-800-263-4433
nature.ca

SWIM
IN A ROCK QUARRY

Affectionately called Stonetown, St. Marys, Ontario, is known for the abundance of limestone buildings in the area. It should then come as no surprise that the town is home to Canada's largest outdoor freshwater swimming pool. The pool is one of two limestone quarries in the area. It was filled with water to become a swimming hole in the 1930s and remains a popular place to cool off today.

Used for more than just swimming, the quarry offers beach volleyball, a water trampoline, two rafts, and a slide. Swimmers can try stand-up paddleboarding or cliff jumping into the water. Tennis courts and the River Walk are across the street, or you can grab a rod and reel and do some fishing.

425 Water St. S
St. Marys, ON N4X 1B6
1-519-284-3090
townofstmarys.com/en/recreation-and-culture/Swimming-Quarry.aspx

FUN FACT

Canada's ninth prime minister, Arthur Meighen, is buried in the St. Marys Cemetery.

IN THE AREA

Canadian Baseball Hall of Fame and Museum
386 Church St. S.
St. Marys, ON N4X 1C2
1-519-284-1838
baseballhalloffame.ca

McCully's Hill Farm
4074 Perth Line #9, R.R. 2
St. Marys, ON N4X 1C5
1-519-284-2564
mccullys.ca

River Valley Winter Tube Slide
4725 Elginfield Rd. (#7 Highway)
St. Marys, ON N4X 1C6
1-519-225-2329
rivervalleygolfandtube.com

St. Marys Golf & Country Club
769 Queen St. E.
St. Marys, ON N4X 1G2
1-519-284-3704
stmarysgolf.com

Westover Inn
300 Thomas St.
St. Marys, ON N4X 1B1
1-519-284-2977
westoverinn.com

JUMP THE RAPIDS
IN A WHIRLPOOL JET BOAT

Niagara Falls is home to incredible waterfalls, and it is also the place to find Class 5 whitewater rapids. Whirlpool Jet Boat tours take you to the edge of some of the most extreme rapids in the world on the seven-mile gorge of the Niagara River. The fast-moving boats perform such tricks as Hamilton 360 turns while they fly across the rough water. As exciting as it is, you don't have to be a daredevil to do it.

You can push your limits and feel the water in your face on a wet jet boat tour. This is an uncovered jet boat where you experience the rapids with all your senses. The covered jet dome boats allow younger children and more cautious individuals to ride the rapids while staying comfortably dry under the dome. Both types of jet boat perform the same stunts and follow the same rapids, and both provide an exciting tour.

Niagara-on-the-Lake location
61 Melville St., Niagara on the Lake, ON L0S 1J0
1-888-438-4444
whirlpooljet.com

FUN FACT

The Niagara River flows fifty-eight kilometres from Lake Erie through Lake Ontario to the Saint Lawrence River, finally emptying into the Atlantic Ocean.

SUNBATHE
ON THE WORLD'S LONGEST FRESHWATER BEACH

You might think that one of the Great Lakes would hold the title of world's longest freshwater beach, but that is not the case. Wasaga Beach, located at the southern tip of Georgian Bay, holds this honour. With fourteen kilometres of wide, sandy beaches and shallow water, there is always room for more sunbathers. Despite being one long beach, Wasaga Beach has many different personalities.

The beach is divided into eight sections, each with its own unique vibe. Beach one is the most touristy section, with souvenir shops, fast food, and bars. Beaches two to four offer cycling trails and picnic areas. Cottages line beaches five to eight, making them quieter spots with fewer amenities.

11-22nd St. N.
Wasaga Beach, ON L9Z 2V9
1-705-429-2516
ontarioparks.com/park/wasagabeach

FUN FACT
Approximately one hundred million lake trout live in Lake Superior.

TAKE A WALK
ON THE GREAT TRAIL

The Great Trail, originally named the Trans Canada Trail, is a series of walkways, roads, and waterways that cross every province and territory in the country. It is twenty-four thousand kilometres long, making it easy to experience some of it but nearly impossible to see it all. It is continually being enhanced and improved.

Much like Canada, the Great Trail is extremely diverse. It spans countrysides and crosses through urban centres. The trail is used by hikers, cyclists, snowmobilers, and commuters. It crosses oceans, travels over bridges, and sprawls through the wilderness. In some areas, the trail is lined with activity and events, while in others it is a quiet, retrospective path. The Great Trail is an excellent analogy for the Canadian people: diverse but connected.

thegreattrail.ca

FUN FACT

In Dawson City, Yukon, you can join the "Sourtoe Cocktail Club." To join, you must finish a drink with a real human toe in the bottom. The motto is "You can drink it fast, you can drink it slow, but the lips have gotta touch the toe."

51

SEE WHALES SWIMMING AMONGST ICEBERGS

The Atlantic Ocean is a playground for many types of whales, making it a popular place to go whale watching. Off the coast of Newfoundland and Labrador is an even more exciting option than simply whale watching: watching whales swim amongst the icebergs off the coast of Fogo Island.

The area is known as Iceberg Alley. The Labrador current pushes icebergs south from Greenland, while the current from the North Atlantic Ocean pushes back. The icebergs turn into massive icebergs that float in the sea near Fogo Island. Whales migrating north pass through this beautiful but nautically treacherous area, providing some of the most stunning whale-watching experiences around. Stick to the shore for viewing, though, as this is where the *Titanic* sank.

FUN FACT

There are no snakes in Newfoundland, but the Narcisse Snake Dens in Manitoba are home to the largest gathering of garter snakes in the world.

52

CHILL
AT A WINTER CARNIVAL

Most Canadians have childhood memories of their school winter carnivals. It was a full day to play outside in the snow, building snowmen, skating, and drinking hot chocolate, but winter carnival fun is not just for children. Winter festivals and carnivals are celebrated across Canada each winter. Talented artists create fantastic ice sculptures, families toboggan down snow-covered hills, and friendly games of hockey take place on local ice rinks, while others practice snowshoeing and cross-country skiing. At some carnivals, you can even learn to build an igloo. No festival would be complete without fantastic food and drinks for all to enjoy. Hot chocolate, hot apple cider, beavertails, poutine, and maple syrup taffy are sure to be on the menu at every Canadian winter carnival.

FUN FACT

The Rideau Canal in Ottawa has the world's longest skating rink in the winter.

WINTER FESTIVALS

Yukon Sourdough Rendezvous
1-867-667-2148
yukonrendezvous.com

Toonik Tyme
tooniktyme.ca

Festival du Voyageur
1-204-237-7692
heho.ca

Winter Festival of Lights
1-866-668-9365
wfol.com

Winterlude
1-844-878-8333
ottawatourism.ca/events/winterlude

Carnaval de Québec
1-418-626-3716
carnaval.qc.ca

53

EXPLORE
GROS MORNE NATIONAL PARK

A place like no other, Gros Morne National Park in Newfoundland is a natural wonder that you must see to believe. Named a UNESCO World Heritage Site, the land offers mountains, streams, beaches, and glaciers. The freshwater fjords lined with towering cliffs are speckled with multicoloured granite rocks. Waterfalls trickle like tinsel off the cliffs. As you wander the hundred kilometres of trails through forests and across streams, wild caribou or moose may be glimpsed in the distance. Towards the coast, tall grass blows in the wind, leading the way to beautiful sandy beaches.

This is an ideal place for personal introspection, connecting with nature, or geocaching with the family, and visitors can explore on their own or use a guide for an inside scoop of the area. The range of different landscapes in the park makes it possible for people of all physical abilities to hike through Gros Morne National Park, where you'll feel as if you've left civilization.

pc.gc.ca/en/pn-np/nl/grosmorne

FUN FACT

Canada has forty-two national parks across the country.

GLENBOW MUSEUM (page 113)

LAKE LOUISE (page 111)

MONT TREMBLANT (page 16)

***WONDERLAND* SCULPTURE** (page 112)

RIPLEY'S AQUARIUM (page 67)

Sean Camp, Lucid Musings

WESTOVER INN (page 73)

HOODOOS IN DRUMHELLER (page 114)

CN TOWER (page 66)

WHIRLPOOL AERO CAR (page 74)

DINO DIG (page 130)

WORLD'S LARGEST DINOSAUR (page 122)

GIRL IN A WETSUIT (page 109)

STANLEY PARK TOTEM (page 109)

ROCKY MOUNTAINEER (page 12)

WHIRLPOOL JET BOAT (page 74)

TONGA LUMINA (page 16)

ROYAL TYRRELL MUSEUM (page 130)

SKI
DOWN A MOUNTAIN

Canadians enjoy a variety of winter sports, including ice hockey, lacrosse, ringette, curling, and, of course, skiing. With snow in every province and territory at some point in the year, cross-country skiing is a sport that can be done almost everywhere that you can find relatively flat ground for just the cost of the ski equipment. Many conservation areas offer ski rentals for visitors who wish to glide across the snowy countryside.

Downhill skiing demands a more specific terrain, with mountains offering the most ideal experiences. The sight of a mountain ski trail may spark fear, but even the most majestic mountain ski lodges offer bunny hills and lessons. For many, the best part of a ski resort is the lodge. The sauna, hot drinks, and warm fireplace are welcoming after a long day on the slopes.

FUN FACT

"Yukigassen" is Japanese for snow battle, and it is the name given to the competitive snowball fights that take place across Canada and the world.

CANADIAN SKI MOUNTAINS

Kicking Horse Mountain Resort
1500 Kicking Horse Trail
Golden, BC V0A 1H0
1-800-258-7669
kickinghorseresort.com

Silver Star Mountain Resort
123 Shortt St.
Silver Star Mountain, BC V1B 3M1
1-800-663-4431
skisilverstar.com

Whistler Blackcomb Ski Resort
4545 Blackcomb Way
Whistler, BC V8E 0X9
1-800-766-0449
whistlerblackcomb.com

Ski Big 3
Banff's three big ski resorts
1-844-754-2443
skibig3.com

Ski Marmot
Marmot Basin
1 Marmot Rd.
Jasper, AB T0E 1E0
1-866-952-3816
skimarmot.com

Blue Mountain Resort
190 Gord Canning Dr.
Blue Mountains, ON L9Y 1C2
1-833-583-2583
bluemountain.ca

Tremblant
1000 Chemin des Voyageurs
Mont-Tremblant, QC J8E 1T1
1-888-738-1777
tremblant.ca

SOAK
IN HOT MINERAL SPRINGS

There are debated benefits to soaking in a steamy hot mineral spring. The natural mineral content of the water is said to have healing powers that extend from nourishing skin to improving respiratory function and soothing aching muscles and joints. Whether there are healing properties is irrelevant once your body is enveloped in the sublime spring. The cool air contrasts with the heat in the water, while the sounds of nature lull you into a deep state of relaxation.

Canada is home to many natural and man-made hot mineral springs. Most hover around 38°C (100°F), which is much warmer than the earth that surrounds them. The sulphur scent of natural springs can be off-putting but is a harmless smell that is easy to overlook once your muscles respond to the pampering of the hot springs.

FUN FACT

The discovery of Banff Upper Hot Springs in the 1880s led to the creation of Canada's first national park, Banff National Park, to protect the hot springs.

HOT SPRINGS

Takhini Hot Pools
KM 10 Takhini
Hotsprings Rd.
Whitehorse, TY
Y1A 7A2
1-867-456-8000
takhinihotsprings.com

Canyon Hot Springs
7050 Trans Canada
Hwy. #1
Revelstoke, BC V0E 2S0
1-250-837-2420
canyonhotsprings.com

Liard River Hot Springs Provincial Park
located at kilometre 765 of
the Alaska Highway
1-250-776-7000
gov.bc.ca/bcparks/explore/
parkpgs/liard_rv_hs

Radium Hot Springs
5420 Hwy. 93
Radium Hot Springs, BC
VOA 1M0
1-800-767-1611
hotsprings.ca/radium-
hot-springs

Banff Upper Hot Springs
1 Mountain Ave.
Banff, AB T1L 1KU
1-800-767-1611
hotsprings.ca/banff-upper-
hot-springs

Miette Hot Springs
Jasper, AB T0E 1E0
1-800-767-1611
hotsprings.ca/miette-
hot-springs

Temple Gardens Hotel & Spa
24 Fairford St. E.
Moose Jaw, SK S6H 0C7
1-800-718-7727
templegardens.sk.ca

PHOTO OPS

HAIDA GWAII TOTEM POLES

Twenty-six ancient and massive totem poles stand guard at the village of Ninstints, Haida Gwaii. This is the largest grouping of Haida totem poles in the area, but such relics dot the landscape throughout the old villages where the Haida people lived. The totems were introduced to the rest of Canada and the world in the 1930s when artist Emily Carr depicted them in her work.

Haida Gwaii, formerly known as Queen Charlotte Islands, is a group of islands on the Pacific Northwest coast that can be reached only by air or ferry. Getting to the totem poles requires a float plane, a charter boat, or booking with a local tour company. The totem poles are in varying stages of decline, and the remaining Haida people choose to leave the totems to decay naturally rather than making attempts to preserve them. With possibly less than a decade left in their life span, the totems will soon be only a memory.

pc.gc.ca/en/pn-np/bc/gwaiihaanas

FUN FACT

The Haida people are divided into two interdependent tribes, the eagle and the raven. They must marry from the opposite tribe, and children automatically become part of the mother's tribe.

57

OLYMPIC CAULDRON

Vancouver, British Columbia, hosted the 2010 Winter Olympic Games. Rather than build a traditional Olympic torch for the games, the city introduced a modern design known as the Olympic Cauldron. This unique piece of architecture consists of four giant poles jutting out of the ground at an angle leading to the cauldron perching at the top. When it is lit from the base of each pole, the result is a burning cauldron surrounded by four smaller flames.

The ten-metre-tall monument has a permanent home in front of Jack Poole Plaza, with the mountains and harbor making a stunning backdrop. The cauldron does not remain lit but is highlighted with artificial lighting to create a stunning image night or day.

1055 Canada Pl.
Vancouver, BC V6C 0C3
1-604-689-8232
vancouverconventioncentre.com/about-us/our-story/olympic-legacy

FUN FACT
The mildest climate in all of Canada is found in Vancouver and Victoria, British Columbia.

THE HANGING GARDEN TREE

A visit to Tofino, British Columbia, offers countless opportunities to photograph the beauty of nature, with rain forests, inlets, and wildlife. Just a water taxi ride away, one particular hike will guide you to a very special chance to photograph at least part of the hanging garden tree.

The tree is eighteen metres wide, so the chances of getting a shot of the entire tree are slim to none, but the experience of standing in the shadow of a two-thousand-year-old western red cedar tree is enough to lead people there. It is believed to be one of the oldest trees in the world as well as the largest western red cedar. The trail has boardwalks that wrap around the tree, without causing damage, so visitors can take in the monumental beauty from many different angles.

tofinohiking.com/hikes/big-tree-trail

FUN FACT

Khutzeymateen Provincial Park is a grizzly bear sanctuary that is home to more than fifty bears.

GIRL IN A WETSUIT

Just off the seawall on the north side of Stanley Park, British Columbia, you will find a statue of a girl sitting on a rock in the water. Often mistaken for a mermaid, the bronze statue is a girl in a wetsuit, hence the name. She was given to the Vancouver Park Board in 1972 by sculptor Elek Imredy, who made the sculpture in the likeness of one of his friends. While many believe the statue was a copycat of Copenhagen's *The Little Mermaid*, the artist denies that claim and says she was created to represent Vancouver's dependence on the sea. However she came to be, *Girl in a Wetsuit* is an iconic Vancouver landmark.

vancouver.ca/parks-recreation-culture/stanley-park.aspx

FUN FACT

All the grey squirrels in Stanley Park are descendants of the eight grey squirrels that came from Central Park, New York City, in 1966.

RAINBOW CROSSWALK
IN DAVIE VILLAGE

Spartacus, a gay holiday guide, recently listed Canada, along with Portugal and Sweden, as the world's most LGBTQ+ friendly travel destination. Evidence of Canadian acceptance is a colourful display at the intersection of Davie and Bute streets in downtown Vancouver's West End. Four rainbow crosswalks form a square at this busy intersection that leads to the LGBTQ+ friendly Davie Village. Painted as a kick-off to the 2013 Pride celebrations in Vancouver, these were the first permanent rainbow crosswalks in the country. Today you can find many permanent rainbow crosswalks in Canada, and many more crosswalks get temporary rainbow makeovers each June in celebration of Pride month.

FUN FACT

Toronto's Pride Festival is one of the highest-attended events in the country and one of the largest Pride events in the world.

61

LAKE LOUISE

The Fairmont Chateau Lake Louise is a grand, picturesque hotel sitting beside Lake Louise, a magnificent sight. Located in the hamlet of the same name, Lake Louise is part of Banff National Park in the Canadian Rockies. From a short distance, the snow-capped mountains and soaring trees reflect off the glassy emerald water of Lake Louise. As you approach the edge of the water, smooth, round rocks lead from the shore into the lake, where they are perfectly visible under the crystalline water. Trails lead around the lake and up the mountains. A teahouse provides a relaxing break from your hike and offers more impressive views. The lake and surrounding area are awe inspiring from every angle. Guests shouldn't leave before visiting the nearby and equally beautiful glacier-fed Moraine Lake.

banfflakelouise.com/lake-louise

FUN FACT

The hamlet of Lake Louise is the highest permanent settlement in Canada.

WONDERLAND SCULPTURE

Calgary, Alberta, has a vibrant urban culture with special value placed on art. Locals showcase their appreciation for the arts through a public art initiative that commits a percentage of all capital building project budgets to public art. The results are tangible, with innovative sculptures and creations coming to life throughout the city. *Wonderland* is one of those pieces.

World-renowned artist Jaume Plensa created *Wonderland*, a twelve-metre-tall wire sculpture of a girl's head. Visitors can step inside the wire piece for a truly unique vantage point and walk around to snap photos from all angles. The piece sits in front of the Bow, which is another eye-catching sight in downtown Calgary. The curvature of the glass building appears to hug *Wonderland*, creating an ideal pairing.

110 6 Ave. SE, Calgary, AB T2G 0G2

FUN FACT

Calgary is known for Chinooks, which are warm winds that blow in and can alter temperatures by as much as ten degrees in a matter of minutes.

IN THE AREA

Calgary Tower
101 9 Ave. SW
Calgary, AB T2P 1J9
1-403-266-7171
calgarytower.com

The Glenbow Museum
130 Ninth Ave. SE
Calgary, AB T2G 0P3
1-403-268-4100
glenbow.org

Stephen Avenue Walk
340 8 Ave. SW
Calgary, AB T2P 1C1
1-403-215 1570
calgarydowntown.com/saw.html

HOODOOS IN DRUMHELLER

Drumheller, Alberta, has a rich coal mining history, an impressive dinosaur fossil collection, and acres of badlands to explore. Within the badlands are natural rock formations called "hoodoos." These oddly shaped rocks are like mushrooms, with their thin pillars topped with wide caps. They were given the name "hoodoos" because they were considered somewhat ghostly, and they are also referred to as "fairy chimneys" and "goblins."

While these pillars with top hats are mystical and the area where they are found is otherworldly, there is nothing supernatural about them. Over millions of years, the rocks have eroded from the base, leaving them with the wider top. Eventually they waste away, and the cap falls to the ground.

traveldrumheller.com/attractions/drumheller-hoodoos

FUN FACT

Drumheller is the dinosaur capital of the world because of the number of fossils found in the area.

CASTLE BUTTE

Beyond the flat countryside of the prairies lies a scene straight out of an old Western movie. The Big Muddy Badlands are a series of badlands that run along Big Muddy Creek through Saskatchewan and Montana. Also known as the "Outlaw Trail," this valley is dotted with cacti and ravines and was once the hiding place of several famous outlaws. Petroforms placed long ago can be discovered on the ground by the discerning eye. The sandstone and red clay ground appears to change colour as you move through the valley.

One distinctive benchmark in the badlands is Castle Butte. Not a castle at all, Castle Butte is a sixty-metre-high land formation that has been used as a landmark for travelers throughout time. Caves that peek out the sides of the structure could have been used by bandits to make a quick getaway, and they can be explored today. Climb to the top of Castle Butte for an outstanding 360 degree view of the badlands.

Big Beaver, SK S0H 0G0
Twenty-two kilometres south of Bengough on Highway 34 and five kilometres west on grid road.
Watch for sign at turnoff.
1-306-268-2909
bengough.com

FUN FACT

Estevan, Saskatchewan, is one of the sunniest places in Canada, with more than 2,500 hours of sunshine a year.

CROOKED BUSH

There's a botanical mystery growing in Alticane, Saskatchewan. A small grove of aspen trees, known as the Crooked Bush, are contorted and deformed in an unnatural way. The mutated trees sit huddled together in a small area and seem to grow at a much slower rate than usual. Despite speculation from scientists and locals, no one knows exactly what caused the trees to twist and wind in such an odd formation. Theories include alien interference, supernatural involvement, or variances in the soil, which is unlikely because there are normal aspen trees just a short distance away. Local folklore about cattle avoiding the trees and people experiencing dizziness when entering the grove only adds to the mystery. Those who want to see for themselves and speculate on the cause can take the short stroll on the boardwalk around the trees.

Alticane, SK S0M 0A0
(306) 549-2331
hafford.ca/crooked-bush.html

FUN FACT

Saskatchewan is home to the world's most northerly sand dunes. These thirty-metre-high sand dunes are in Athabasca Sand Dunes Provincial Park.

BANNOCK POINT PETROFORMS

Petroforms are man-made shapes and patterns created on the ground by placing rocks or boulders as the outline. Like petroglyphs, which are images carved into stone, petroforms can be thousands of years old. Inukshuks, which are vertical rock formations in the shape of a human, are a type of petroform, as is the famous Stonehenge in Wiltshire, England.

The Bannock Point petroforms are found in Whiteshell Provincial Park, Manitoba. The prehistoric petroforms are made in the shapes of turtles, snakes, and even humans. These spiritual petroforms were placed by First Nations people, and while they are a wonder to see and photograph, they should not be touched or altered.

MB-307, Division No. 1
Unorganized, MB
1-204-369-3157
mhs.mb.ca/docs/sites/bouldermosaics.shtml

FUN FACT

Inukshuks are used as a directional markers to indicate danger or mark significant locations.

CHELTENHAM BADLANDS

Caledon, Ontario, has a geological treasure that is usually found farther west. The Cheltenham Badlands run along the Niagara Escarpment and were once the base of an ancient lake or sea. The land is a series of small, smooth hills and gullies, best described as a rolling landscape. Iron oxide in the earth creates a red rust shade across the area, with green ribbons running throughout.

The Cheltenham Badlands have been damaged by large numbers of tourists and overuse and were once closed to the public entirely. They are open once again, but they cannot be accessed from the Bruce Trail as they once could. There is now a dedicated parking area and a sanctioned viewing area that protects the badlands from further damage but allows everyone to see their beauty.

Caledon, ON L7C 0K6
1-800-665-4453
ontariotrails.on.ca/trails/view/cheltenham-hills

FUN FACT

Nearby Toronto has more than 1,600 parks and more than two hundred kilometres of walking and biking trails.

FAIRMONT LE CHÂTEAU FRONTENAC

Often mistaken for a castle, the Fairmont Le Château Frontenac is a hotel that overlooks Old Québec. Visible through most of the fortified city, the chateau sits atop the hill like a guardian of the ancient town. It is not surprising that this regal piece of architecture holds the Guinness World Record for the most photographed hotel in the world.

Built by the Canadian Pacific Railway in 1893, the hotel is now a National Historic Site of Canada, and visitors to the area can take a tour even if they are not hotel guests. The views of the city and the Saint Lawrence from the hotel are as extraordinary as the hotel itself.

1 rue des Carrières
Québec City QC G1R 4P5
1-418-692-3861
fairmont.com/frontenac-quebec

FUN FACT

The Fairmont Banff Springs Hotel in Alberta is also often mistaken for a castle. It is referred to as the "Castle in the Rockies."

HORSESHOE FALLS

Canada's Horseshoe Falls at Niagara Falls, Ontario, is an obvious bucket list item for many people. The enormity of the falls, roar of the water flowing from the river and crashing into the gorge, and unique horseshoe shape are all selling points for the area.

Walking along the sidewalks that line the river while feeling the mist from the falls is the most common way to see them, but other options provide different views. Hornblower Niagara Cruises deliver you as close to the base of the falls as possible. Journey Behind the Falls guides you through tunnels, where you can look out from directly behind the falls, and takes you to a platform beside the roaring waters. The new zipline is a thrill-seeking experience over the falls, and a helicopter tour provides a rare overhead view. The Skylon Tower and the Skywheel give visitors two more unique vantage points for viewing the falls.

FUN FACT

In 1901, a sixty-three-year-old schoolteacher made history as the first person to go over the falls in a barrel and survive. Her cat also survived the trip.

IN THE AREA

Bird Kingdom
world's largest free flying indoor aviary
5651 River Rd., Niagara Falls, ON L2E 7M7
1-905-356-8888
birdkingdom.ca

Butterfly Conservatory
2565 Niagara Pkwy.,
Niagara Falls, ON L0S 1J0
1-877-642-7275
niagaraparks.com/visit/attractions/butterfly-conservatory

Casino Niagara
5705 Falls Ave.
Niagara Falls, ON L2E 6T3
1-888-325-5788
casinoniagara.com

Clifton Hill
home to midways, restaurants, shops, wax museums, and haunted houses
4960 Clifton Hill
Niagara Falls, ON
L2G 3N4
1-905-358-3676
cliftonhill.com

Fallsview Casino Resort
6380 Fallsview Blvd.
Niagara Falls, ON L2G 7X5
1-888-325-5788
fallsviewcasinoresort.com

Niagara Falls History Museum
5810 Ferry St., Niagara Falls, ON L2G 1S9
1-905-358-5082
niagarafallsmuseums.ca

Whirlpool Aero Car
3850 Niagara Pkwy.
Niagara Falls, ON L2E 3E8
1-877-642-7275
niagaraparks.com/visit/attractions/whirlpool-aero-car

THE WORLD'S LARGEST LOBSTER

Around the world are larger-than-life roadside attractions, and Canada is no exception. Giant displays of local industry can be found in cities and provinces across the country. One unforgettable showpiece is the World's Largest Lobster in Shediac, New Brunswick. This fifty-five-tonne sculpture (with a thirty-five-tonne base) was built by the late Winston Bronnum. It was put on display in Shediac, also known as "The Lobster Capital of the World" because of the booming lobster fishing industry that the town is famous for. The orange-and-black lobster is perched on a pedestal made for visitors to climb up and get their photos taken next to the enormous lobster claws.

229 Main St.
Shediac, NB E4P 2E3
1-506-532-7788
shediac.ca

FUN FACT

New Brunswick has the warmest saltwater beaches north of Virginia.

OTHER LARGER-THAN-LIFE ATTRACTIONS IN CANADA

World's Largest Totem Pole
Alert Bay, BC V0N 1A0
atlasobscura.com/places/world-s-largest-totem-pole

World's Largest Hockey Stick & Puck
2687 James St.
Cowichan Community Centre
Duncan, BC V9L 2X5
atlasobscura.com/places/worlds-largest-hockey-stick-puck

World's Largest Dinosaur
Drumheller, AB
T0J 0Y0
1-866-823-8100
worldslargestdinosaur.com

Mac the Moose
Tourism Moose Jaw
450 Diefenbaker Dr.
Moose Jaw, SK S6J 1N2
1-306-693-8097
tourismmoosejaw.com/#/mac/tutorjet

Husky the Muskie
Lakeview Drive
Kenora, ON P9N 1S4
1-807-467-2000
ontariotravel.net/en/listing/Husky-the-Muskie/201305

Jumbo the Elephant
Info Centre @ L&PS Station
605 Talbot St.
St. Thomas, ON N5P 1C6
1-519-631-1680 ext. 4132
railwaycitytourism.com/jumbo.html

71

THE BOTTLE HOUSES

In Cap-Egmont, Prince Edward Island, is a unique set of buildings set amongst tranquil gardens. The Bottle Houses are three buildings designed and constructed by Édouard T. Arsenault in the 1980s. Arsenault collected and recycled glass bottles that he then used to build the Bottle Houses.

Twelve thousand bottles were used to create the first structure, a six-gabled house with colourful patterns directing light throughout. Next, a tavern came together with eight thousand bottles, not including the ones on the bar! The chapel was the last bottle house to be built. Ten thousand green, white, and orange bottles make up the walls and decor inside. The gardens are equally beautiful, and a quaint white lighthouse also makes an excellent photo subject.

6891, Road 11, Cap-Egmont, PE C0B 2E0
1-866-671-2987
bottlehouses.com

FUN FACT

The PEI artist got the idea to build his glass house after his daughter sent him a postcard of a similar home in British Columbia.

PEGGY'S POINT LIGHTHOUSE

Peggy's Cove is a popular destination because of the picturesque coast, quaint buildings, and Peggy's Point Lighthouse. One of the most well-known lighthouses in the area, the Peggy's Point Lighthouse was built in 1915 to be a beacon for vessels approaching the fishing village. The red-and-white pillar sits on top of smooth granite that disappears under the surface of the water.

The beautiful stature of the lighthouse on the rocks has drawn many curious visitors too close to the water's edge on the slippery rocks, sending them into dangerous waters. Take your photos from a safe distance so that you can find more charming views in the area. With more than 160 historic lighthouses in the province, you are sure to make some more discoveries.

Located just an hour from Halifax, Peggy's Cove and the lighthouse may be reached on Highway 333 or Highway 103 from Halifax to Exit 5 and then Route 333.

peggyscoveregion.com

FUN FACT

Local legend says that Peggy's Cove was named after the sole survivor of a shipwreck, who washed up there, suffering from amnesia and remembering nothing but her name.

FACE IN THE WINDOW
AT ST. PAUL'S CHURCH

A somber and somewhat eerie reminder of the Halifax Explosion of 1917 is the face in the window at St. Paul's Church. The church sits several kilometres away from the location of the blast, which was caused when an ammunition ship exploded, but the explosion was so powerful that it was felt as far away as Prince Edward Island. At St. Paul's Church, the blast embedded a piece of window frame into the arch of the entranceway, where it remains today. The west gallery window of the church clearly shows the silhouette of a person. Legend says that a deacon was standing in the window when the explosion took place, and his image was permanently marked on the glass. The fate of the deacon is unknown, but his image remains for all to see.

1749 Argyle St.
Halifax, NS B3J 3K4
1-902–429-2241
stpaulshalifax.org

FUN FACT

The Canadian Museum of Immigration in Halifax is Atlantic Canada's only national museum.

TYRANNOSAURUS

HISTORY AND CULTURE

LEARN ABOUT DINOSAURS
AT THE ROYAL TYRRELL MUSEUM

The Royal Tyrrell Museum in Drumheller, Alberta, has the largest collection of complete dinosaur skeletons in the world as well as many other fossils and archaeological finds. A hub for paleontologists and dinosaur fanatics, the museum is relatively close to Dinosaur Provincial Park, the largest archaeological site in the world for dinosaurs from the Late Cretaceous period. Everything found on the archaeological digs at Dinosaur Provincial Park is taken to the Royal Tyrrell Museum. Aside from having incredible dinosaur displays throughout the museum, it is also an active scientific research facility. The museum offers school programs, camps, and junior dinosaur digs for younger visitors.

1500 N. Dinosaur Trail
Drumheller, AB T0J 0Y0
1-403-823-7707
tyrrellmuseum.com

FUN FACT

Alberta has a dinosaur named after it, the Albertosaurus, a tyrannosaurid theropod from the Late Cretaceous period.

HEAR SWEET SOUNDS
AT STUDIO BELL

Studio Bell is The National Music Centre in Calgary, Alberta. A stunning architectural site, the building is home to the Canadian Music Hall of Fame, where there are displays of instruments, costumes, and other memorabilia from such artists as Shania Twain and the Barenaked Ladies. The roots of Canadian icons and music genres are explored throughout.

Recording studios are available for use in the museum, which also holds concerts and hosts educational programs. Visitors can test their own musical skills at various interactive stations, including using motion to create sound and showing off your talent with instruments provided. Get the inside scoop by booking a guided tour.

850 4 St. SE, Calgary, AB T2G 1R1
1-403-543-5115
studiobell.ca

FUN FACT
The world's first UFO landing pad was built in St. Paul, Alberta, in 1967 as a Centennial project.

VIEW
THE DUCK LAKE MURALS

Duck Lake, Saskatchewan, has a deep First Nations history that is displayed for all to see on several murals located around the town. This outdoor gallery depicts the local historical events that involved the Metis and early settlers, such as the Battle of Duck Lake that started the North-West Rebellion in 1885. Each piece tells a different story of the West, the Metis, and the pioneers who came to the land. Various local artists contributed to the Duck Lake murals, including Brian Seesequasis, Glen Scrimshaw, Laureen Marchand, and Ru Huang. Visitors can learn more about the history of Duck Lake and the murals by visiting the Duck Lake Regional Interpretive Centre.

Town Office in Duck Lake
Duck Lake, SK S0K 1J0
1-306-467-2277
ducklake.ca/visitors/murals.html

FUN FACT

The province of Saskatchewan has approximately one-hundred thousand lakes.

SPEND A DAY
AT THE ROYAL SASKATCHEWAN MUSEUM

The Royal Saskatchewan Museum is a single museum separated into two locations, Regina and Eastend. The museum was opened in 1906 after a boulder was discovered with petroglyphs on it, and the locals put it on display. That first display led to others, and today the museum shares artifacts and information about Saskatchewan's natural history and aboriginal culture.

The Eastend location opened as a T. rex discovery centre to honour Scotty, the largest Tyrannosaurus rex in the world. Named after the bottle of scotch that was shared in celebration of his discovery, Scotty is a sixty-five-million-year-old monumental skeleton that was found in Saskatchewan.

2445 Albert St.
Regina, SK S4P 4W7
1-306-787-2815
royalsaskmuseum.ca

FUN FACT

Scotty the T. rex lived to be approximately thirty years old, making him the longest living T. rex on record.

DISCOVER

THE CANADIAN MUSEUM FOR HUMAN RIGHTS

The Canadian Museum for Human Rights in Winnipeg, Manitoba, is the world's first museum dedicated to human rights. It is currently the only museum of its kind, both contextually and architecturally. The unique design of the building draws visitors in, and the stories inside capture their attention. The mandate of this national museum is to inspire a global dialogue and promote respect for others.

Exhibits in the museum are not limited to Canadian experiences. There are displays and artifacts relating to human rights violations around the world. The museum shares information about civil rights leaders from many countries and notable women in history. It delves into the tragedies of the past, such as the Japanese internment, with the hope of avoiding similar tragedies in the future. Events, films, speaking engagements, and discussion circles all take place inside the museum.

85 Israel Asper Way, Winnipeg, MB R3C 0L5
1–877-877-6037
humanrights.ca

FUN FACT

A part of Mars was named after Winnipeg because of the cold climate in both places.

79

PAY A VISIT
TO PARLIAMENT HILL

Anyone who enjoys history, politics, or incredible architecture will enjoy a visit to Parliament Hill in Ottawa, Ontario. The stately buildings with their decorative arches and wrought-iron fences are the first indication that important business takes place behind the walls. Once inside, you can discover how Parliament works and attend actual debates taking place.

The Parliament of Canada's knowledge centre is the Library of Parliament, one of the most iconic Parliament buildings. Dedicated government employees spend time in the library working to preserve and support democracy in Canada. The Parliament buildings can be seen on guided tours or by touring on your own.

lop.parl.ca

FUN FACT

Ottawa has dedicated three areas in the city for graffiti artists to legally showcase their work.

SEE
A SHAKESPEAREAN PLAY

The Stratford Festival Theatre had humble beginnings under a circus tent in the early 1950s before becoming the grand amphitheater it is today. The stage is brilliantly built with a removable balcony, protruding platform, trapdoors, several acting levels, and eight major entrances. This allows for quick scene changes and the ability to achieve most set designs. Most famous for Shakespearean plays, the festival has regular showings of many types of theatre, including musicals. Famous actors such as Christopher Plummer, Colm Feore, and Megan Follows have all graced the stage in Stratford over the years.

Plays are also held at the Avon Theatre, the Studio Theatre, and the Tom Patterson Theatre, all of which are part of the Stratford Festival. The organization also offers workshops, tours, and acting camps.

1-800-567-1600
stratfordfestival.ca

FUN FACT

The Avon Theatre in Stratford has placed a bronze star in the ground on the spot where Justin Bieber played guitar for coins as a child.

IN AND AROUND STRATFORD

Anna Mae's Bakery & Restaurant
home-cooking restaurant and bakery
4060 Perth Line 72
Millbank, ON N0K 1L0
1-519-595-4407
annamaes.ca

Gallery Stratford
54 Romeo St. S.
Stratford, ON N5A 4S9
1-519-271-5271
gallerystratford.on.ca

Hamlet of Shakespeare
antique shopping galore
Highway 7/8 east of Stratford
visitstratford.ca/hamlet-of-shakespeare

St. Jacobs Farmers' Market & Flea Market
878 Weber St. N.
Waterloo, ON N2J 4A9
1-519-747-1830
stjacobsmarket.com

Stratford Perth Museum
4275 Huron Rd.
(Highway 8, just west of Stratford)
Stratford, ON N5A 6S6
1-519-393-5311
stratfordperthmuseum.ca

Wildwood Conservation Area
3995 Line 9, RR #2
St. Marys, ON
N4X 1C5
1-519-284-2292
wildwoodconservationarea.ca

GO TO
THE HMCS *HAIDA* NATIONAL HISTORIC SITE

The HMCS *Haida* is a distinguished tribal-class destroyer ship that served in the Royal Canadian Navy during World War II, the Korean Conflict, and the Cold War. The ship was named after the Haida people from Western Canada and is now on display and available to explore in Hamilton, Ontario. Visitors can walk the decks, pretend to be at sea, and imagine what it was like to serve on what is dubbed "Canada's most fightingest ship" because she sank more enemy ships than any other allied vessel. The HMCS *Haida* was designated the flagship of the Royal Canadian Navy, and it is the last surviving tribal-class ship of the twenty-seven originals.

Pier 9, 658 Catharine St. N., Hamilton, ON L8L 8K4
1-905-526-6742
pc.gc.ca/en/lhn-nhs/on/haida

FUN FACT
Hamilton, Ontario, is the waterfall capital of the world.

IN AND AROUND HAMILTON

African Lion Safari
1386 Cooper Rd.
Cambridge, ON N1R 5S2
1-519-623-2620
lionsafari.com

Canadian Warplane Heritage Museum
9280 Airport Rd.
Mount Hope, ON L0R 1W0
1-905-679-4183
warplane.com

Dundurn National Historic Site
610 York Blvd.
Hamilton, ON L8R 3H1
1-905-546-2872
hamilton.ca/attractions/hamilton-civic-museums/dundurn-national-historic-site

Royal Botanical Gardens
680 Plains Rd. W.
Burlington, ON L7T 4H4
1-905-527-1158
rbg.ca

Halton County Radial Railway
13629 Guelph Line
Milton, ON L0P 1B0
1-519-856-9802
hcry.org

LOOK FOR PETROGLYPHS
IN PETROGLYPHS PROVINCIAL PARK

Petroglyphs are indigenous rock carvings, often of people, animals, or spiritual symbols. Petroglyphs Provincial Park in Woodview, Ontario, has the largest known concentration of First Nations petroglyphs in Ontario. Known as "The Teaching Rocks," it is a sacred site where you can discover petroglyphs of turtles, snakes, humans, birds, trees, and more. A carving of a human, taller than the rest, with a head that appears to be the sun, is considered by some to be a representation of the Great Spirit. It is believed that the stones were carved by the Algonkian people between 900 and 1100 AD. The park also offers great opportunities for wildlife viewing, which can be continued at the Peterborough Crown Game Preserve that borders Petroglyphs Provincial Park.

2249 Northey's Bay Rd., Woodview, ON K0L 3E0
1-705-877-2552
ontarioparks.com/park/petroglyphs

FUN FACT
Peterborough was the first Canadian city to get electric streetlights.

83

VISIT
THE TRENT-SEVERN WATERWAY NATIONAL HISTORIC SITE

The Trent-Severn Waterway has a series of heritage canals and locks that connect Lake Ontario and Lake Huron. The 386-kilometre waterway is an inland passage that takes you through several lock stations. These revolutionary locks work like an elevator, using the water levels to raise or lower vessels before they move to the next section of the passageway. Visitors can watch the locks operate from land or take a boat tour and experience them from the water.

The area is particularly stunning in autumn, with the leaves putting on a colourful show. The Peterborough Lift Lock Visitor Centre provides more information about the locks and can direct visitors to nearby lumber camps and farms.

2155 Ashburnham Dr., Peterborough, ON K9J 6Z6
1-705-750-4900
pc.gc.ca/en/lhn-nhs/on/trentsevern

FUN FACT

The Peterborough Lift Lock is the highest hydraulic lock in the world, with a rise of sixty-five feet.

EXAMINE
THE MARCONI NATIONAL HISTORIC SITE

In December 1902, Guglielmo Marconi changed how the world communicates, with the first official wireless message across the Atlantic Ocean. The Marconi National Historic Site of Canada is in Table Head in Glace Bay, Nova Scotia, at the location of this first transmission. Marconi chose Table Head because there was flat ground he needed for the towers as well as an unobstructed view over the Atlantic Ocean. The towers remain at the site today along with a modern amateur radio station and a museum that displays the history of Marconi's work. When visiting the Marconi National Historic Site, take out your smartphone and snap a photo of the place that made it possible to share the experience with the world.

15 Timmerman St., Table Head, Glace Bay, NS B1A 5M7
1-902-842-2530
pc.gc.ca/en/lhn-nhs/ns/marconi

FUN FACT

Halifax's famous Old Town Clock has been keeping time since 1803.

TOUR
OAK ISLAND

Oak Island, Nova Scotia, is most famous for the legend of the Oak Island money pit. Treasure hunters have been searching for the money pit and other artifacts, such as the Holy Grail and the Ark of the Covenant, since the nineteenth century. It was formerly talked only about amongst treasure hunters and Nova Scotians, but a reality show called *The Curse of Oak Island* brought the legend to living rooms everywhere.

Oak Island is privately owned, but a limited number of historical walking tours are offered on the island each year. Book as far in advance as possible because these popular tours fill up quickly. The Oak Island Interpretive Centre is free to browse and learn more about the island, the treasure, and the discoveries that have been made thus far.

Oak Island Tours Inc.
Western Shore, NS B0J 3M0
oakislandtours.ca

FUN FACT

Legend says that seven men will die on Oak Island before the treasure is found. To date, six people have died while searching for the Oak Island treasure.

TRAVEL
THE HARTLAND COVERED BRIDGE

New Brunswick is home to many covered bridges, and they are all referred to as “kissing bridges.” This dates back to the horse and buggy days, when opportunistic young men would train their horses to stop halfway across the bridge and allow a young couple to share a kiss before continuing on. The Hartland Covered Bridge is the world’s longest covered bridge, providing more than one chance to steal a kiss on the trip across.

Now a National Historic Site, the Hartland Covered Bridge is 390 metres long and was built in 1901. The bridge crosses the Saint John River from Hartland to Somerville, a journey that could previously be made only by ferry. A pedestrian path was added to the bridge in 1945.

365 Main St., Hartland, NB E7P 2N1
1-506-375-4357
tourismnewbrunswick.ca/Products/H/Hartland-Covered-Bridge-National-Historic-Site.aspx

FUN FACT
New Brunswick has more than sixty covered bridges.

GO
TO GREEN GABLES

The story of Anne of Green Gables holds a special place in the hearts of many Canadians. Lucy Maud Montgomery introduced Green Gables to the world in 1908 through her beloved novels. The author was so inspired by the beautiful landscape of her home province, Prince Edward Island, that she made it the setting of her stories about the outspoken red-headed orphan. Today, fans of Montgomery and Anne can visit Green Gables and see exactly where she was when she wrote the books.

Green Gables is located in Cavendish in the Prince Edward Island National Park, and visitors can pretend they're Anne by putting on braids and a straw hat before they explore the Haunted Woods and stroll along the Balsam Hollow Trail described in the novels.

8619 Cavendish Rd., Cavendish, PE C0A 1M0
1-902-963-7874
tourismpei.com/green-gables-house

FUN FACT

More than fifty million copies of *Anne of Green Gables* have been sold worldwide.

VISIT
AN ANCIENT VIKING VILLAGE

Along Newfoundland's Great Northern Peninsula is an ancient Viking village called L'Anse aux Meadows. This UNESCO World Heritage Site looks a little like something out of the shire, with mounds of grass-covered huts and windows peeking out from below. Hobbits have never graced this land, but Norse Vikings made it their home around the year 1000. They are believed to have come from Greenland before settling in Newfoundland, and this is the only Norse Viking encampment in North America outside of Greenland.

The camp was discovered by archaeologists in 1968. It is open for tours, and visitors can see original artifacts from the camp and talk to character Vikings on-site. A Viking trade depot has been re-created nearby.

Division No. 9, Subd. D, NL A0K 2X0
1-709-458-2417
pc.gc.ca/en/lhn-nhs/nl/meadows

FUN FACT

Newfoundland has its own time zone that is thirty minutes ahead of Atlantic time.

Photo by Christine McNaughton
lifeonmanitoulin.com

ROAD TRIPS

JOURNEY UP
THE SEA-TO-SKY HIGHWAY

Taking the Sea-to-Sky Highway from Vancouver to Pemberton is a relatively short road trip at under two hundred kilometres, but with so many possible stops along the way, it can turn into a three-day trip if you desire. There are provincial parks and lookouts along the way, and stopping to walk across the Capilano Suspension Bridge is a must. And it would be unheard of to get that close to Whistler and not make a side trip to do some skiing or hiking.

British Columbia's coast is home to some fabulous golf courses, and there is scuba diving at Porteau Cove Provincial Park. Squamish is an excellent place to stop and bike or walk the trails. With so many lakes, mountain lookouts, pubs, and restaurants, your trip will be one for the books.

tourismvancouver.com/activities/itineraries/sea-sky-highway-weekend

FUN FACT

The world's longest unsupported cable car is in Whistler.

MORE STOPS ALONG THE SEA-TO-SKY HIGHWAY

Furry Creek Golf and Country Club
150 Country Club Rd.
Furry Creek, BC V0N 3Z2
1-604-896-2224
furrycreekgolf.com

Shannon Falls
Squamish-Lillooet D, BC V0N 1T0
1-800-689-9025
exploresquamish.com/trails-routes/shannon-falls

Brackendale Eagles Provincial Park
Brackendale, BC V0N 1H0
1-519-826-6850
env.gov.bc.ca/bcparks/explore/parkpgs/brackendale_eagles/

Scandinave Spa Whistler
8010 Mons Rd., Whistler, BC V8E 1K7
1-604-935-2424
scandinave.com/whistler/en

DRIVE THE DEMPSTER HIGHWAY FROM DAWSON CITY TO INUVIK

The Canadian Territories are the most remote parts of Canada, with empty highways and scenic views. This quiet charm is the reason to take a 740-kilometre summer road trip down the Dempster Highway from Dawson City, Yukon, to Inuvik, Northwest Territories.

The drive will take you to the North Fork Pass. This is the first crossing of the Continental Divide. At a high elevation, the views from here are phenomenal. As you continue along the Dempster Highway, you will grab photos at mile markers and border crossings, travel on ferries, get amazing views of the Mackenzie River and Campbell Lake, and stop for a tour of Fort McPherson. Wildlife sightings are almost guaranteed. The approximate eight hours of driving can be broken up into as many days as you see fit.

dempsterhighway.com

FUN FACT

The Klondike Gold Rush began in Dawson City in 1896 when more than ten thousand prospectors came to the area in search of gold.

VENTURE
FROM VULCAN TO HEAD-SMASHED-IN BUFFALO JUMP

The trip from Vulcan to Head-Smashed-In Buffalo Jump is perfect for Trekkies who also appreciate nature. Begin in Vulcan, Alberta, a town that embraced the name and became an homage to *Star Trek*. In town is a Vulcan Tourism and Trek Station, a bronze bust of Leonard Nimoy as Spock, and an official *Star Trek* Walk of Fame. True Trekkies will be able to discover more *Star Trek* hidden gems as they wander the town.

Once the nerd in you is satisfied, take Highway 23 south for about an hour to Fort MacLeod. Stop here and visit the Fort Museum before carrying on to Head-Smashed-In Buffalo Jump World Heritage Site. Here you can see the cliff that was used as a buffalo jump by the First Nations people and learn the Blackfoot history.

townofvulcan.ca

Head-Smashed-In Buffalo Jump World Heritage Site
275068 Secondary Hwy. 785, Fort MacLeod, AB T0L 0Z0
403-553-2731
headsmashedin.ca

FUN FACT
Vulcan, Alberta, holds an annual Trekkie convention called Vul-Con.

PERUSE
THE WORLD'S LARGEST FRESHWATER ISLAND

Manitoulin Island, Ontario, is the world's largest freshwater island. There are three ways to get to the island: drive along Highway 6 and across the world-famous swing bridge, take the MS Chi-Cheemaun ferry from Tobermory to South Baymouth (May to October only), or fly into one of the two airports on Manitoulin Island.

If arriving by car, continue along Highway 6 to the east until you reach Manitowaning, where you can visit the Assiginack Museum Heritage Complex and learn more about the history of the island. See the Manitowaning Lighthouse and the SS *Norisle* and enjoy some time on the beach.

A marked tourist driving route called the Great Spirit Circle Trail will guide you towards many excellent landmarks on the island. You can follow that or take a self-guided tour around the island to see many historical lighthouses and galleries and enjoy scenic views.

manitoulintourism.com

FUN FACT
Manitoulin Island has 108 freshwater lakes.

STOPS IN MANITOULIN ISLAND

Assiginack Museum Heritage Complex
125 Arthur St., Manitowaning, ON P0P 1N0
1-705-859-3905
assiginack.ca/assiginack-museum-heritage-complex

Bridal Veil Falls
Kagawong, ON
gowaterfalling.com/waterfalls/bridalveilmanitoulin.shtml

Centennial Museum of Sheguiandah
10862 Hwy. 6, Island, Sheguiandah, ON, P0P 1W0
1-705-368-2367
manitoulin-island.com/museums/centennial_museum.html

Great Spirit Circle Trail
5905 Hwy. 540, M'Chigeeng, ON P0P 1G0
1-705-377-4404
circletrail.com

Lighthouses
explorethebruce.com/things-to-do/lighthouses

Old Mill Heritage Centre and Post Office Museum
15 Old Mill Rd., Kagawong, ON P0P 1J0
1-705-282-1442
manitoulin-island.com/museums/
transportation_museum.htm

Ojibwe Cultural Foundation
15 Hwy. 551, M'Chigeeng, ON P0P 1G0
1-705-377-4902
ojibweculture.ca

93

COMMUTE THROUGH THE PRAIRIES
ON THE TRANS-CANADA HIGHWAY

This trip is approximately one thousand kilometres from Swift Current, Saskatchewan, to Winnipeg, Manitoba. Beginning in Swift Current, visit the art gallery and the museum. Do some hiking, shop, or play a round of golf before heading east. Along the way, stop in Moose Jaw and explore the Tunnels of Moose Jaw that were once used by smugglers. Next, spend the night in Regina and see the Sports Hall of Fame, Saskatchewan Science Centre, and RCMP Heritage Centre the following day.

The next leg of the trip is nearly four hours long across the flat plains of the prairies, but you can stop and stretch your legs in any of the small towns you pass before reaching Brandon, Manitoba. Here you can visit the Manitoba Agricultural Hall of Fame and go to the Riverbank Discovery Centre before leaving for Winnipeg, where you can see the Royal Canadian Mint, Lower Fort Garry National Historic Site, and many craft breweries.

FUN FACT

The Trans-Canada Highway is the world's longest highway at 7,604 kilometres.

TRAVEL THE HIGHWAY 60 CORRIDOR

OF ALGONQUIN PROVINCIAL PARK

Algonquin Provincial Park is a source of pride for nature-loving Canadians, particularly in its home province, Ontario. The Highway 60 Corridor passes through fifty-six kilometres of the southern portion of the park. Starting at the west gate, the corridor passes the Whiskey Rapids Trail, where you can watch the Oxtongue River rapids. The nearby Hardwood Lookout is a scenic one-kilometre loop trail, and farther along the highway you will arrive at the Algonquin Art Centre, which features wilderness artists from the area. Camp at Canisbay Lake for the night.

Your second day on the corridor will take you to more hiking trails, lakes, and lookouts. Stop for a picnic at East Beach Picnic Pavilion, and if you want to camp another night, check out Kearney Lake. Before leaving Algonquin Provincial Park, be sure to stop at the Algonquin Logging Museum.

algonquinpark.on.ca/visit/camping/highway-60-corridor.php

FUN FACT

Algonquin Provincial Park is the only provincial park that allows industrial logging.

TREK
AROUND THE GASPÉ PENINSULA

The Gaspésie, or Gaspé Peninsula, is along the south shore of the Saint Lawrence River in Quebec that extends into the Gulf of Saint Lawrence. To fully experience the trip, allow yourself a week to drive around the coast. An excellent starting point is Île Verte to see Quebec's oldest lighthouse. Farther inland, the Matapedia Valley offers salmon fishing and many heritage homes. Other recommended stops on the peninsula include Miguasha National Park, paddling on the Bonaventure River, fishing in Forillon National Park, and taking in the Musée acadien du Québec and Bioparc Wildlife Park. Réserve faunique de Matane offers guided excursions to view wildlife, such as bears and moose.

The cherry on the top of the Gaspésie is Percé Rock. This huge sheer rock formation sits in the Gulf of Saint Lawrence off Percé Bay. It is one of the world's largest natural arches located in water and is a natural icon of Quebec.

quebecmaritime.ca/en/road-trips-and-getaways/the-bas-saint-laurent-gaspesie-tour

FUN FACT

Canada's name comes from the Iroquois word for village, "kanata."

IN THE AREA

Bioparc
123 Rue des Vieux-Ponts, Bonaventure, QC G0C 1E0
1-866-534-1997
bioparc.ca

Forillon National Park
1238 Boul de Forillon, Gaspé, QC G4X 6T9
1-888-773-8888
pc.gc.ca/en/pn-np/qc/forillon

Île Verte Lighthouse
2802, Chemin du Phare, L'Isle-Verte, QC G0L 1L0
1-418-898-2730
phareileverte.com

Musée acadien du Québec
museum
95, Avenue Port-Royal, Bonaventure, QC G0C 1E0
1-418-534-4000
museeacadien.com

Miguasha National Park
231 Route de Miguasha O, Nouvelle, QC G0C 2E0
1-800-665-6527
sepaq.com/pq/mig

Réserve faunique de Matane
wildlife reserve
Rivière-Bonjour, QC G0J 2R0
sepaq.com/rf/mat

BE AMAZED
ON QUEBEC'S WHALE ROUTE

With thirteen different whale species swimming in the estuary and gulf of the Saint Lawrence, Quebec is great for whale watchers. This 1250-kilometre whale-watching trip will take an average of four to six days driving along Quebec's eastern coast.

Begin the trip in Tadoussac, Quebec, and head northeast along the coast to Blanc-Sablon, stopping at any of the whale-watching tours listed on the whale route. Each stop offers a chance to see any of the thirteen whale species, including the blue whale, the humpback whale, and the beluga whale, by boat tour, zodiac, or sea kayak. You will also notice other wildlife, lighthouses, and shipwrecks along the way. You may also want to visit the Cap-de-Bon-Désir Interpretation and Observation Centre and Vauréal Canyon and Falls.

tourismecote-nord.com/en/discover-our-region/must-see/the-whale-route

FUN FACT

Peanut butter dumplings are a gastronomical specialty in Montreal.

CRUISE
THE CABOT TRAIL

The Cabot Trail in Cape Breton is another trip that could be done in a day, but three to five days provide enough time to take in the natural beauty and make some stops along the way. Both directions around the loop offer beautiful scenery, but the clockwise direction is a little less daunting for the driver. The Cabot Trail has several opportunities for hiking, biking, and going to the beach, as well as boat tours for whale watching. The Sunset Art Gallery has one-of-a-kind wood carvings and paintings by local artists. Other stops around the loop include the Alexander Graham Bell National Historic Site, Big Spruce Brewing, and Uisge Bàn Falls Provincial Park. Cabot Cliffs and Cabot Links golf courses are both highly rated clubs that can be found on the Cabot Trail.

cabottrail.travel

FUN FACT

Residents of Halifax, Nova Scotia, are referred to as Haligonians.

IN THE AREA

Alexander Graham Bell National Historic Site
559 Chebucto St.,
Baddeck, NS B0E 1B0
1-902-295-2069
pc.gc.ca/en/lhn-nhs/ns/grahambell

Big Spruce Brewing
64 Yankee Line Rd.
Baddeck, NS B0E 1B0
1-902-295-2537
bigspruce.ca

Cabot Cliffs and Cabot Links
18 Cabot Ln.
Inverness, NS B0E 1N0
1-902-258-4653
cabotlinks.com

Cape Breton Highlands National Park
hiking, wildlife, beach
37639 Cabot Trail
Ingonish Beach, NS
B0C 1L0
1-902-224-2306
parkscanada.gc.ca/capebreton

Glass Artisans Studio & Gallery
45054 Cabot Trail
North Shore, NS B0C 1H0
1-888-262-6435
glassartisans.ca

Pleasant Bay
hiking, whale watching
pleasantbay.cabottrail.com

Sunset Art Gallery
15856 Cabot Trail
Chéticamp, NS, B0E 1Z0
1-902-224-1831
sunsetartgallery.ca

Uisge Bàn Falls Provincial Park
hiking and waterfall
715 N. Branch Rd.
Baddeck, NS B0E 1B0

WANDER AROUND
FOGO ISLAND

Fogo Island, 120 kilometres north of Gander, Newfoundland, is a small island that leaves a big impression. The island is home to many fishing villages that offer extraordinary views even when shrouded in fog. After taking a ferry to the island, you can seek out lighthouses, boat tours, and many hiking trails, such as the Brimstone Head, Lion's Den, and Fogo Head trails.

The Fogo Island Inn is an architectural wonder that you will want to see or stay in for a night or two, giving you time to see Oliver's Cove and visit the art gallery and museums. Whales, seals, and caribou may all be spotted on your visit, depending on the time of year.

townoffogoisland.ca

FUN FACT

The people of Newfoundland took in more than 6,600 people who were stranded at Gander International Airport on September 11, 2001. Documentaries and a Broadway play have been made about the experience.

IN THE AREA

Bleak House Museum
32-36 North Shore Rd., Fogo, Fogo Island NL A0G 2B0
1-709-266-1320

Brett House Museum
36 Brown's Point Rd., Joe Batt's Arm, Fogo Island
NL A0G 2XO
1-709-266-1320

Fogo Island Gallery
210 Main Rd., Joe Batt's Arm, NL A0G 2X0
1-709-658-3444
fogoislandarts.ca

Fogo Island Inn
210 Main Rd., Joe Batt's Arm, NL A0G 2XO
1-855-268-9277
fogoislandinn.ca

Marine Interpretation Centre
77-79 Harbour Dr., Seldom, Fogo Island NL A0G 3Z0
1-709-266-1320

DEFY GRAVITY
ON THE MONCTON MAGNETIC HILL

The Magnetic Hill in Moncton, New Brunswick, has baffled many travelers through the years. As you approach the base of the hill in a car, rather than increasing power to go upwards, you are seemingly pulled up the hill. Test the theory by putting your car in neutral and watch it roll uphill. Even cyclists can stop peddling at the bottom of the hill and still arrive at the top, but the secret behind the magnetic hill is not magic or a lack of gravity. It is simply an illusion. While it appears to be uphill, it is actually downhill.

The Moncton Magnetic Hill is a fun side trip just fifteen minutes from downtown Moncton, forty-five minutes from the famous Hopewell Rocks and seventy-five minutes from Prince Edward Island.

2846 Mountain Rd., Moncton, NB E1G 2W7
1-800-363-4558
tourismnewbrunswick.ca/Products/M/Magnetic-Hill.aspx

FUN FACT

An area in the Hudson Bay region has less gravity than the rest of the planet.

IN THE AREA

Fundy National Park
8642 Rte. 114
Alma, NB E4H 1B4
1-506-887-6000
pc.gc.ca/en/pn-np/nb/fundy

Magic Mountain
150 Magic Mountain Rd., Moncton, NB E1G 4V7
1-506-857-9283
magicmountain.ca

Magnetic Hill Zoo
125 Magic Mountain Blvd.
Moncton, NB E1G 4V7
1-506-877-7722
mhzooeducation.com

Shediac Bay Cruises
60 Pointe-du-Chêne Rd.
Pointe-du-Chêne, NB E4P 4V8
1-888-894-2002
shediacbaycruises.ca

USVA Spa Nordik
774 Front Mountain Rd.
Moncton, NB E1G 3H3
1-855-SPA-USVA
usva.ca

CROSS
THE CONFEDERATION BRIDGE

The scenic Confederation Bridge connects Prince Edward Island to New Brunswick. At nearly thirteen kilometres in length, it is the longest bridge in the world to cross ice-covered waters. The curved bridge is considered one of Canada's top engineering achievements of the twentieth century. It took four years to build from the mid- to late '90s, with more than five thousand people working on it during that time.

A trip across the Confederation Bridge takes approximately ten minutes, and at the highest point you will be sixty metres above sea level. A cruise ship may even pass under the bridge while you cross. When lit up at night, the bridge creates a stunning scene between the provinces.

1-888-437-6565
confederationbridge.com

FUN FACT

Prince Edward Island is the smallest province and has just two cities: Charlottetown and Summerside.

IN THE AREA

Cavendish Cliffs
Cavendish, Prince Edward Island
tourismpei.com/green-gables-shore/cavendish

Confederation Centre of the Arts
145 Richmond St.
Charlottetown, PE C1A 1J1
1-800-565-0278
confederationcentre.com

PEI Brewing Company
96 Kensington Rd.
Charlottetown, PE C1A 5J4
1-902-629-2739
peibrewingcompany.com

St. Dunstan's Basilica
45 Great George St.
Charlottetown, PE C1A 4K1
1-902-894-3486
stdunstanspei.com

Summerside Farmers Market
250 Water St.
Summerside, PE C1N 1B6
1-902-432-8396
summersidefarmersmarket.com

Wyatt Historic House Museum Thumb Three
85 Spring St.
Summerside, PE C1N 3E8
1-902-432-1296
culturesummerside.com

ACTIVITIES
BY REGION

ACROSS CANADA

TERRITORIES

BRITISH COLUMBIA

ALBERTA

SASKATCHEWAN

MANITOBA

ONTARIO

QUEBEC

NEW BRUNSWICK

NOVA SCOTIA

PRINCE EDWARD ISLAND

NEWFOUNDLAND AND LABRADOR

ACTIVITIES
BY SEASON

SPRING

SUMMER

FALL

WINTER

INDEX